An Eloquence of Time and Space

D1555298

by **James Wylder**
Illustrated by Olivia Hinkel

additional content by
Taylor Elliott
Andrew Gilbertson

Cover by
Olivia Hinkel and Alyssa Fifer

DEDICATION

To Verity Lambert,
and every person who has made Doctor Who possible over
these 50 years.

Also available by James Wylder:

Cascade

An eclectic swirl of poetry that shifts through phases building to a final Cascade of words.
Also contains the full-length play "Paper Gods."

and coming soon to print and Kindle:

Cryptos

The popular 2011 play finally comes to print! A pair of Cryptozoologists investigate an isolated religious cult, searching for a monster that may or may not exist...

God Save the Pres.!

A play about Zoey, an ordinary girl from Colonial America, who is accidentally sent forward in time to the modern day where a pair of political schemers hatch a plan to run the 200 year old teen for President.

The Dark and Splendid Diary of Danielle Simpson (and other tales)

A girl takes out the horrible struggles of her life through fiction in this novella, also featuring a selection of James Wylder's short fiction.

One-Act Septology

James' complete short plays come to print at last, featuring "The Tragedy of Hilarious: A Comedy.", "Butterfly Machinery", and "Rex Stout Rings Again!"

Death and Doubling Cubes

In this thrilling Sci-Fi novel, Jhe Aladdin's father found a way to merge his memories with another person's by accident, and now a being has come looking for Aladdin, seeking to gain infinite knowledge.

CONTENTS

ACKNOWLEDGMENTS

This book would not be possible without the generous help and support of Josephine Smiley, Olivia Hinkel, Alyssa Fifer, Taylor Elliott, Andrew Gilbertson, Bob Baker, David Koon (who created the character of Graelyn Scythes), Bryan Swan, Elizabeth Tock, Ellie Fairfield, Nathan P. Butler, Brandon Derk, Kayla Snabl, Aubrey Minnick, The Black Crow on Main,

And everyone who backed the Kickstarter to make this book possible.

Thank you.

James Wylder

An Invitation to Adventure....
Did you ever see the stars?
Oh, I know you did, and I know you do.
They're always up there, except when the Phalanx turned
them all off--
But never mind that, there's places to go, and wonders to
see.

Fields that shimmer like silk in the wind,
fires on candlesticks that line tables
waters that lap at your toes, and then flee from you scared,
and so many skies with so many stars

and you can see those stars on any night, if the clouds are
clear enough
sitting by yourself, eating crisps, wandering the heavens in
your mind

but you know whats better? You can see it all. Star by star,
footfall by footfall
running through life like you've always dreamed,
but with a hand to hold
you might trip when you're running and then it comes in
handy!
But also, it'd be your hand
and I want you to share that adventure, see those stars, so
come on!
Are you gonna take my hand or not?

1 ELDER WHO

An Eloquence of Time and Space
Doctor... Who?
That funny old bloke in the junkyard?
Out of his place and out of his time
Never one for words or questions
But we're always about queries
and we're always about works
eloquently asking him,
from where he comes
and where he'll go,
and what place will stop the journey

but for now the mist rolls away,
across the forsaken Foreman's scrap
where we'd been known to rust
and there a Blue Box waits out the chill
with scarce a mention of the strange words
of where it starts and where it goes
and who lives inside it too
(from Gallifrey to Trenzalore)
we all ask.... Doctor... Who?

1.1 An Unearthly Child

She was so distant
like hands and inch from holding
her gaze on the circumference of molecules
and the voodoo of Circe
wrapped up in her palm
only almost in contact
like a fiber selected off a cloth for analysis
or witchcraft

she hurtled through my birth and death
and chuckled at my protoplasm
taking lunch with Darwin
and tea with Moses
on a casual Sunday and tomorrow

she slipped through our fingers
unable to be grasped/out of reach
but never once out of time

1.1.5 100,000 BC

what kind of a man moves though us
passes through our Genesis
to find the revelation of our
stunned awe
laughing in fits of godlike wonder
he mashes our composure
with trinkets from Olympus

Smiting down ants
magnifying the broken glass
of his temples of a time machine

1.2 The Daleks

I hadn't really begun
till it roared to life
in a forest of carbon and ashes

holed up in shells of cooking wear
surviving through storms
of nibbling Chernobyl
eaten away to fanaticism
and a screaming sunset

still your city lies shining
dripping in mercury
and flooding the future
with eloquent oddities
enraptured in catchphrases

pushing along cliff faces and drops
and fake food schemes
to cut you out of your shells
like turtle soup
breathless and withering under a mat

till you are at once
gone forever
and begun for good
returning soon enough
when you were wiped out to the last can

1.3 The Edge of Destruction

At the end of all things
we're liberated from the footsteps we took
by shattered glass
pieced back together a million times

timelords vs. humans
time vs. skin
our very faith versus our deepest fears
the kidnapped mortals vs. the vengeful gods

turning smashed reality
into a crew

1.4 Marco Polo

First soldier down
among the videotapes
with the ark of the covenant
you nest
sitting down for tea
in China
with a man who traveled
like a TARDIS
on two feet

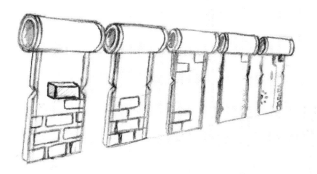

1.5 The Keys of Marinus

Brick by brick / to acid shores
we build the key / we send you unlocked
to unlock worlds / and certainty
from open trials
where the white haired are strung up
to lands where all that's seen is snow
and unlocked portents
dripping in rubber faced lies

and one piece is here
and one piece is there
and brick by brick
we build the key
to unlock worlds and certainty

1.6 The Aztecs

blood and bone
bridge the sun to the soil
with a lot of heart
beating outside your body
under a prayer

till you change it all
and pull down pyramids
to have teatime and crucifixion
on Mesoamerican Soil clinking your colonialism "Slainte!"
while before you the daggers dig deep
to drown dialogue
in their heated eyes
cloaked in Jaguars
to keep out the dawn

1.7 The Sensorites

Alone in the tumbleweed nothingness
with so far out on either end
to stretch your eyes and hand
and touch nothing but starlight

there is a hand on the windowpane

1.8 The Reign of Terror
Freedom through Razor Blades
       -and raucous inferno-
Liberte, Egalite, and burn away
freedom for all through blood, blood, blood
and lock away the other ones
for humane tea time
with Madame Guillotine

so shoot him in the jaw
if he takes too much power
and get back to England
with no allowance
for rings or plumed hats
to lead them astray

and someday
we shall have

Liberte, Egalite, Fraternite

#2
So ends a year
in stars so formless and deep
clenched to static tubes
for Hartnell and his keep

2.1 Planet of Giants

to be an ant
is to be a giant
and tear through the dirt
carrying high tide leaves
and loose yourself in the
footsteps that print the ground
which you see as canyons

and what if we were your
footprint walkers?
Would we tremble
at the force
of your
Sunday perambulations

2.2 The Dalek Invasion of Earth

I

You clenched your hand so hard
to let go is dreaming
your life running down to pool
and flat away with your frock coat
when your family is forgotten

II

bodies in the river
their creeping stench nothing
to the children poking for scraps
eyes turned up feral
hungry at the crumbling sky

III

Saucer
Milk dish, teatime
a clink of cups
a smile, biscuits
two laughs, caked in disrepair
as we fade to/
Saucer
cutlas in the sky
lamentation of the weary
holding up in tea pots
wreathed in the sludge of bodies

IV
Wheelchair
rolling to the sound
of deaf and dumb blasts
castrating the hope of millions
with unearned platitudes
and a fear of flight

V
Aufiderzein she would say
Aufiderzein to the drowning teapots
burning in their skyriver
like Ragnor's Pyre
No loner to whisk us away
but to leave us in place
boxed in on all of time
a 8 legged hex on a thousand strands of fate
cutting loose the one last thread
tying us to the womb

2.3 The Rescue

unemploying
the masks
of our expectation
to rip away rubber
and reveal our own rescue
saved from monstrosity
with hung-headed rashness
and lamentations
over fang-toothed pets

2.4 The Romans

Months and months
of grapes and froth
on couches and coastlines
unaware of the villa-ny
of daggers and Nero

when far off cities burn
for comic effect
under the bread and circus skyline
and the far far reach
of the notes of a baldfaced lyre

2.5 The Web Planet

we are all weird
and nothing is really so human
as to blur the lines of humanity
metamorphosing into butterflies
and cracking our crystallizes
which we webbed ourselves
for this strange strange land
in this strange place
for everyone to see
our bug-eyes decency

2.6 The Crusade

Saladin was draped in courtesy
running current to distrust
as lines of crusade currency
send prisoners to dusk

an old man veils adopted girls
to curtsey male at court

to tremble at a Lionheart
the pain of war, defers

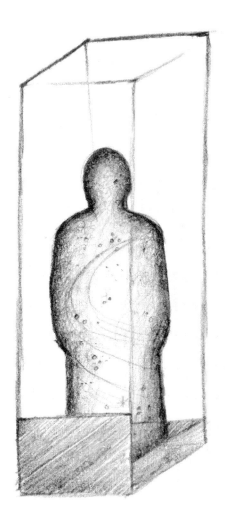

2.7 The Space Museum
we are / lost
in glass / memorials
a relic / not worthless
of our / advent
appat / ures
ite / mised
ever hungered / for no gold
in revolution / to impatience
and waiting

2.8 The Chase
round and round and round
and round and round and round
and round and round and round we all go
stopping at nowhere
sinking ships and
slipping our foes like trashcans
from worlds on water to cities of bone
making friends 20 minutes at a time
with no guide book
working our way through history
leaving only snapshots
to remember our long vacation

2.9 The Time Meddler
Knowing better than clocks
and pointing with blindfolds at row boats
we wave the incense
for king and causality
thinking we are king makers
when we are only tinkerers for gunsmiths
saving the earth
one imagined threat guillotined at a time

3.1 Galaxy 4
suns rise and fall
and we make our own bedfellows
not for war, but for its sake
blood, letting us salute the flag
to bomb out our zodiac symbols
so no one can give us advice
till all we are are beehive haircuts
and go-carts
putting around each other
putting at the sun
for the sake of solemnity

3.2 Mission to the Unknown

There's nothing to be done
when the Doctor Doesn't come
you can fight and
sink your fangs in all you want
you'll still die
and try and try to run
there's nothing to be done
when the Doctor doesn't come

3.3 The Myth Makers

I, Cassandra
Eye, of Troy
Foresaw this all, if you would hear me
of wily Odysseus and Agamemnon
of a wooden horse
and our misery
but... did I foresee this?
A wooden box of bluest blue
turning the gears of our war
making our deaths into myths

but will our burned walls
and tortured bodies
be anything but
storybooks
when the horror still shines in my
crumbling vision

3.4 The Daleks' Master Plan

1.
How could a plan so good
be so wrong?

2.
Death – he died, she dies
a short lived lifespan
destined for mortuaries

3.
kindle the forest
with infection light
dwindle the trees
till we poison the night

4.
we're going away-
-running to allies-
-that no one can trust-
-not even their leverage-

5.
Airlock
she was in the
Airlock
she was supposed to be leverage
and she was supposed to laugh
come Christmas time
with friends for gods she never knew
but she went into the Airlock
and she will praise neither
Apollo or Jesus
as her bloated corpse floats
in an infinite misunderstanding
of who is divine

6.
He was the Hero
with a square jaw
and a gun hip
vaporized by a woman in a catsuit
just like he was supposed to be

7.
 silver jumpsuits
and tree fur claws
guardians of storm clouds
watering plants that speak like men
and waste the day
waiting for walking soup cans

8.
Christmas – raise a cheer to Christmas
on the Feast of Stephen
with a toast to new friends
and old friends
and the hope for a year anew

9.
What is a plan
with out a touch of risk
what is a risk
without a chance
to win something extreme

10.
So maybe we betrayed
everyone
along the leylines
we always liked energy guns
more than looking up "allies"
in dictionaries.

11.
Foiling the Foliage and Foe allegiance
marching with no feet
fierce and adrenalineless
rolling along till

12.
The End.
When the plan comes together
and fades out
so does her last breath
and the hope
that he could save us after all

3.5 The Massacre of St. Bartholomew's Eve

There was a time
when seeing yourself in the mirror
wasn't followed by bullet holes
but that time has long since passed
into the rats that scurry
to dig up their arrow in bones
tilling the soil with rats teeth
and gunpowder
unable to hear our concessions
over the battle-cry

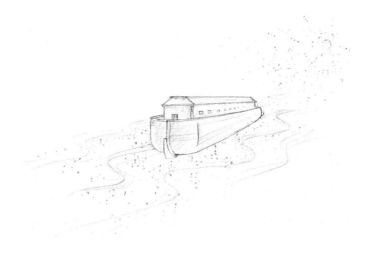

3.6 The Ark

there was once a man named Noah
or was he someone else?
Who built a contraption to float on
was it a boat? Or did it float on a sea of moondust?
Rocking along in solitude
2 by 2
with genetic compulsion
to complete the circle of life

3.7 The Celestial Toymaker

I am in the employ
of towers of Hanoi
and hide bound to hopscotch
for not is more serious
than serial storytelling
at the bark of your mindgames
where you push the swing
one last time

3.8 The Gunfighters
galloping off
with their hands in their gunbelts
gallant gunfighters
signal the O.K.
To Doctor the Holiday
with lead
and dissent

James Wylder

3.9 The Savages

To Stephen:
Goodbye, into that great solitude
of cave and service
surrounded by those you could save
fostering days with sweat and
endless work by campfires
telling the story of an old man
shunted from place to place
as the savages cradle their young
and you look up to the stars
you dropped from
into the palm of peace

3.10 The War Machines

To Ben and Polly:
Thrust upon the unexpected
replicants of
more popular t-shirt stains
you charge into the world full bore
never so brave
as to stand against the wondrous horror
the mod and the sailorsuit
hands together
unlikely allies
against the machines of war

4.1 The Smugglers

Knives and rum
and whiskey to come
pierced in with the hoops
and hidden in carts
thicker than water
but not so thick
as to burden ourselves
with any allegiances
beyond the alloys
we don't take for altruism

4.2 The Tenth Planet

To balance his cosmos
the Earth must have its counter-weight
dipping into the fabric of space
and slicing out organs
to feed to the frigid lord
that sucks you dry
from morning till shriveled up sleep

that is the Mondas
the sleep you haven't got
cracking your eyes to open
to the light of iPods

and along the leylines
we sooth-say
with middle school note passing
of prophecy
screaming as Cassandra
when they come to take our faces off

ebbing away with patience
and the laws of black magic
we cast our lots into the show
as the other world ends
and the face of the prophet changes
to make way for new life
away from leylines

2nd Doctor

4.3 The Power of the Daleks
Power Level: One

Everything can never remain
even Daleks' metal stain
we lose whats old but stay the same
to lull us into tea with cower
I am your servant, so plain
everything can never remain
surging with a fluxing power
could they love this horrid game
we lose whats old but stay the same
and our faces turn so ever dour
as new feet step down the lane
everything can never remain
the ring fits neither finger nor hour
but that hand anything could tame
we lose whats old but stay the same
destroying the shell of the deep so sour
eyed in the dark, with new mirth and pain
everything can never remain
we lose whats old but stay the same

Power level: Two

His face is the same, but totally different.
There is no ring on his finger to kiss
and it won't slide on
Keeping himself hidden
under a veil of confusion
lining his pockets with a
500 year diary
and the scrolls of Alexandria

4.4 The Highlanders

call yer redcoats while ye can
and rush away their Highland plan

Marching cross the fields in gangs
and so in fear the churchbells rang
and a noble laddie piping for the clan

Still can burn up in the pan
when so many noble songs were sang
still the Scottish men did hang

4.5 The Underwater Menace

Atlantis is cracking
lost under the echoes
of Plutarch and sonar
spreading its gills
as the seas becomes a kracken
waiting to close down its last city
to make room for fish hatcheries

4.6 The Moonbase

Returning again
from their search for the philosopher's stone
eternal life eludes them
as we wake from drowsy delirium
to see faeries and ghosts
of the darkest dreams of our fate

4.7 The Macra Terror

stomping at claws
and the crustacean catalog
of barreling down to the depths
fleeing yet another monster
more ready than ever to
drag us down with it

4.8 The Faceless Ones

Take off landing
smoldering passengers
with tray snacks and peanuts
waiting to vanish
and cut off the demeanor
of a lost cause
with internal investigations mustache
and the endless liftoff
where the men and ladies
have no more faces to me
than the last batch

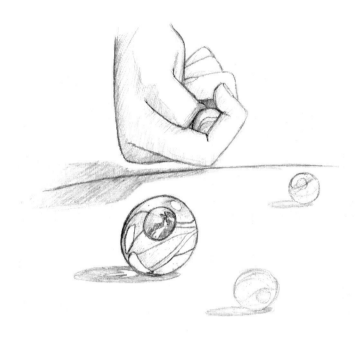

4.9 The Evil of the Daleks
The best way to kill an emperor
is through playtime

there is an image backwards
and in it, time enough
for the mansion to build and fall
and through it more-
-faces of friends, fallen and past
and new ones whose petticoats
will grace your stagnant decks
tossing and turning
in the shimmer of a sky
with no up or down

and we put our party hats on emperors
to see their clothes in their vampire reflection
and lay out hopscotch for wheelchairs
moving square by square
a revolution of children's games

5.1 The Tomb of the Cyberman

you are opened
in single serving packets
bubble wrapped and shipped
into extra solar sarcophagi
burning incense to pharaohs
doing the Egyptian down the hallway
dancing with Doctors
who damn you to
irrelevancy
with hieroglyphics
and a predisposition
to de-nile your crown
and exile your
hierophant hierarchy
with arcane science textbooks

5.2 The Abominable Snowmen

And we sing our darkening hymn
born of pasts that couldn't begin
lord of memories, thoughts, genetically
nothing is there at all.

Yog-Soggoth, mind to be
hear these halls eternally
cough your ledger, gnash your pleasure
horrid my mind, soon to be

chanting on, though monster and climb
Himalayas, Yetis, or time
sing orb praises
still amazes
burning our thoughts to dust

Yog-Soggoth, mind to be
Great Intelligence, tis thee
tear our heads off, scream our leisure
slaves of your path are we

5.3 The Ice Warriors

Its passing

As the time goes by and we lose
our bits to snowflakes I miss
you in the frigid mire
where the sackmen wear skins
and loot the surface of civilization
for its leftover trinkets
when we are all leftovers

though us

nothing is possible without science
every chart burned into our equations
every computer running behind
freezing its CPUs off
into the old ice age

to take back

Mars. Where there were once empires
and claws gripped hooded
trophies and gnashed thin lips
as hell froze over, predictably as fits

marching through tundras
a snake in their voice
killing and chilling and leaving with choice
and speaks at

the soil

that we so despaired
and we hold it back so to breathe
one more retching breath
and drag ourselves through
scorn Martian blood for earth again
and hold back the ice age of imagination
and birth again ideology
a lost memory

That we sacrificed for concubines of
smog and disposable napkins

5.4 The Enemy of the World

You're so full of your own intent
sunning on rocks by the riverbed
I thought I'd return the compliment
somehow I see you with imminent faces
but the looks don't mask the depths of that head
you're so full of your own intent
Chernobyling notions with hunkering bases
such a clever man for so many dead
I thought I'd return the compliment
but how many sleeves shave how many faces
can you keep the world or your own mouth fed?
You're so full of your own intent
the world is far more than a long list of places
begging to be led
I thought I'd return the compliment
so have this gift of infinite spaces
spiraling out in the stars till zed
you're so full of your own intent
I thought I'd return the compliment

5.5 The Web of Fear

"Yog-soggoth mind to be
hear these halls eternally
swiftly orbs descend and fall
Darkness gapes its jaw on call"
-Hymn to the Great Intelligence

Scatted remains of the bird on the tree
wrapped up in silk, plum pudding for me
biting your thoughts and breaking your bones
squatter of brains and churner of thrones

making your daydreams and hopes for its home
cutting out figures of all of your kin
stringing them up
party of sin
dome cup its fingers

right over your ears

-listen-
-you'll hear it-
-drawing your fears-

5.6 Fury from the Deep
let go in the sleeping seaweed
where hands sink down
and we murmur bubbles
grasping fro the hint of sunlight
as down to the deep
we escape,
venting the year
since she saw her father
pass into a deeper ocean

Sinking
      down
         and
            down

               we

             go

burying our hatchet deep
and leaving behind the orphan
on a home
as new as the current
that whisks her away

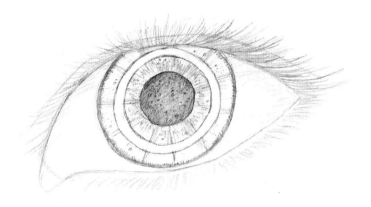

5.7 The Wheel in Space

Rotating around roundels
starring at starlight mathematics
with those blue eyes
in greyscale
another turn
and you're hiding in trunks
waiting for the everlasting
piece of retribution

But it all ends in rerun

6.1 The Dominators
Arms swing swing
to the crystal bling
as you bobble along
don't you sing

kill and destroy
the world is a toy
as you hobble along
its all just a play

you think that you'll be elevated
in stead you'll be educated
as you hobble along
you'll be dominated

6.2 The Mind Robber

Memory lies
on the face of pages
where we open up
to curl into corners
with Gulliver and friends
climbing Rapunzel's hair
into the white nothing
only we can fill
with ink and a dream

6.3 The Invasion

1

Converted with a lazy eye
and throw back moonboots
we radio in our disgust
half awake to climb the tower
to subway stations and rocket ships
training along with squirming muses
by future tech girls

2

A man's world
with testosterone guns
and big cigars
tucked in shirts and berets
fine trimmed mustaches
brimming with chins raised and square jaws
outdone by a girl in a catsuit
with a calculator cranium

3

Glamboot thugs
missiles launch
defeating the thick wires
of industry and malice
with a photo-shoot and feminism

6.4 The Krotons

Re constructable defeat
and never failing victory
building your bodies
out of wine glasses
and your plans in tinfoil
still, you stood above the rest
and silenced so many
marching on threads, in on
the last great name in destiny

only to crack under pressure
like children in the crystal shop

6.5 The Seeds of Death

You rasp
like a fungal infection
with too few digits
to open the pill bottle
you cough it up
through forest and field

drowning the earth
in flashing lights
up and down the corridors
sure to be drowned
in the heyday of rocket fuel

slowed down only by Ares
and the light of a cold, cold, sun

6.6 The Space Pirates

Harsh
cold
Vapor Trails
in a broken
Nonagon

stealing away your breath
in a broken magnetism
just before the end

6.7 The War Games

1.

They put their plebeian plaques to horses
and rode out standard
they put their muskets muzzled
and let them bark with smoke
kept on their long leashes
forgetting the trees they're roped on
hounding history
 hell, they're heroes
wading into their coffins
 tripping into the mist

2.

you could see for
centuries
upon horizon hill
handling the moment of
sunrise
with thick hide gloves
and disco glasses

3.

<u>Machinery of Mind</u>
She raised her hand Hermione High
and her friend demonstrated
regulating mind control
with the half turn of gears
and refrigerator magnets

4.

<u>SIDRAT</u>
She is hollow
a flower unwatered
on the windowsill
while lovers kiss
she bounces through time
not to the laughter of a hobo
but with the silence of tears

5.

Warchief
Dear Doctor Please,
we could beat these
ol' bullies from back home
an empire land, though time enjambed
why do you look so cold?

6.

How do you stop someone
who can hold you with a breath
their fog on the windshield
a crystal cave
binding you to your feet
with spurs of inhibition

7.

No help is coming
with out saying goodbye
to all your wanderings
knowing that the end
comes at the price
of every bold dream

8.

Homeland
these skies were oh so orange
darting under them with a palate
licking your lips red, green, blue
as the color rolls down from the sky
drowning you in the incapability of home

9.
Is it my flower print dress?
Its still in my drawer, unworn...
could it be the laundry?
No, empty hampers abound.
My schedule is free,
the station still turns in the dark
no errands to run
no deeds to be done

so why do I feel I've forgotten something important?

10. You can't make me
go to the face off
ering myself up
scaled into techno
color splitting me a
part in
to pie
ce

s
I'll see you again when
I put my skin back on

3rd Doctor

7.1 Spearhead from Space

Pouring out like plastics
into a skin hide mold
moving your mouth
around vowels
like you bought your tongue at the butchers

silently modeling apparel
man, akin to all
a foreigner
confusing mustaches
with curls

still hidebound though
to baby dolls
popping out of machine-work
into the fabric
of opera capes and incompetence
tramping though forests for glow sticks

to rave away birth
with a Doctor's touch

7.2 Doctor Who and Silurians

Don't forget we weren't here first
we slew the landowner
for buried talents
still under our feet
waking up now to negotiation
and the inevitable genocide

feathers for scales
and scales weighed down
with hardened white guilt

7.3 The Ambassadors of Death

of course across the moon
they stumble
bouncing in Apollonian shoes
infiltrating Troy
in unhuman splendor

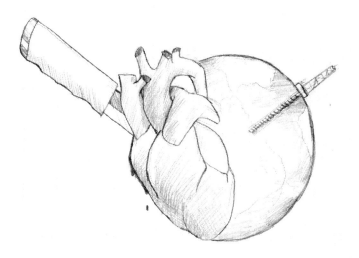

7.4 Inferno

Burning with imitation
and eye patches
we sweep through causes
to find we weren't so different
in the knife in our hearts

8.1 Terror of the Autons

crushing you cushions
comfy chair was deadly
can't trust the fuzz
cause they're alien Autons
absolutely antithetical
to anything but a
most Masterful will

Polar
opposites
of Positively
monstrous degree

8.2 The Mind of Evil

change him now
to preposterous degrees
giving up that right
when its convenient
tumbling away prisoners
down the chute
to waste them away
and pick their brains
like punishment enough
was no just fruit

8.3 The Claws of Axos

one for all
And all is one
camaraderie
in the claws
of a friendship so powerful
it has to only look in the mirror

8.4 Colony in Space

Let off the hook by the jailers a bit
storming though the Universe in purple and glam
once more in the TARDIS, close your eyes and savor it
you'll be grounded again in only a bit

Sealing away doomsday weapons for plowshares
and making the crops grow
with the aid of aliens

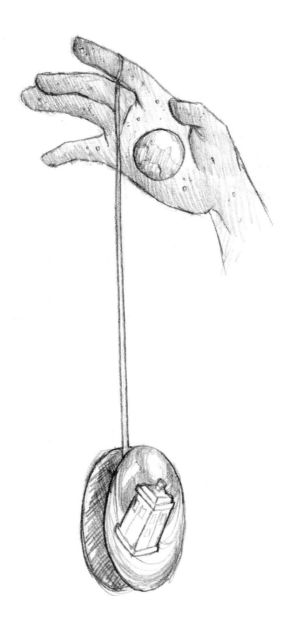

8.5 The Daemons

Horns in Holes and witches in white
all across England's Countryside
old helms from barrows crack the land
and we put bullets in our swords
to update the land of monstrosity
with maypoles and machine guns

casting stones into runes
to read all the horror scopes
and admit
to devilry
when even canary cars are witchcraft

9.1 Day of the Daleks

<u>The Life of Og</u>

There was a child born
under cold moons
whose mother grunted
and rubbed his wailing face
with the god's oil
lifted up on
the seven matron's hands
and passed on through the years
he grew, and soon learned
the names of the rocks and plants
and not to hunt the Sycomote Bat
to kill the Musak, burn the hide
and how to wrestle, beat, and bite
the time till masters came
to buy him up and take him off
from the cold moon sky
he kissed his mother and his mate
and worked for tin cans
who habitate in time
to knock out opera capes

so Og was strong and took his lead
and dreams of his toes
in the brown and green pebbles
under chartreuse clouds
addled and stormed
under eldritch blue sheer
with only one moon
he faces his face
and there were lifetimes
and mothers and kisses
and rocks and skies
and bellows
and now he is just vapor
as the man in the Opera cape
tilts his gun down
towards the rocks

9.2 The Curse of Peladon
Negotiation
Kings and nations
working off of stranger beings
But who could do better
when you have a velvet coat that shade
in service of the king?

9.3 The Sea Devils

The last time you saw them
they were cousins
lost to the world,
and kicked out like scum
who owns the earth?
And who owns the sea?
Laying their claims before humanity.

9.4 The Mutants

Looking down on the world
with scorn and treachery
unable to feel with that much
jackboot up yer leg

marching in rotating time
to remove the men
turning the world to mutants again

9.5 The Time Monster

Chronos!
Keeper of time!
God, and lord in the land where the fishes sleep
ignore its sinking, ignore the last batch
for the queen decrees lovers
In time, with a catch
Chronos!
The Greek, the Master, I here
oh no, that's another.
For Atlantis, I fear.... Again.

10.1 The Three Doctors

Up on a Street, near Coal hill school
We all walked into nothingness
And everything floated past us on wings of paper planes
floating where no one had sacrificed everything

And after all this time, he's all together,
all three with their neckties and coats and pomp
A Doctor for the Ages
glittering away
From the crotchety old youngest
to the middle aged clown
to the glam rock caper
here's how it went down:

In the days before time, time was invented
black holes were discarded so TARDISes were plenty
and one was lost in the ruins
not by coal hill, but a hill he couldn't climb
drowning in nothingness
lost in time

Now we're all back together,
and nothing fades out
held in place by a memory
but aren't we all, with out doubt?

Here goes the memory of all of our friends
Of Hartnell, or Troughton, of Pertwee
All love to them

10.2 Carnival of Monsters

Bottled and Corked
in every conceived vintage
they stir and crumple and writhe
waiting in miniature
to take bites out of moon
and take up the moonlight
into the glowing belly
of television monstrosities

10.3 Frontier in Space

You can't fight a war
without willing opponents
get them on the same page
and you can kill with the best of them

trade agreements
arms races
races wars
and prisons
slice away the last shreds of your humanity
for a bit of landmass
and the right to sputter away another soul into dust

but its all just a game
played behind the scenes
by the forces for whom war cannot seem
to ever be wrong so now we go on to the....

10.4 Planet of the Daleks

cast in shadows of clear
huddle through the jungle
with spears of plungers
and spend your time hunting tigers
made of steel
and immune to eyes
running away planetside

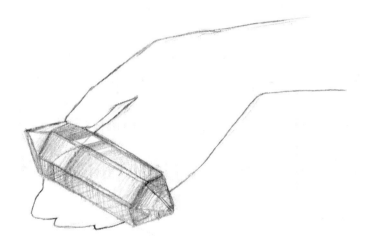

10.5 The Green Death

To Jo:

If I could have told you, Jo,
I would have remembered to mention your brilliance
to put on that smile and march in like you own the universe
well you could, Jo
you could
with your man and your life
and the whole world ahead of you
anything you do, you'll rough the world up
just hold onto that life
and don't expect my face
I can't say goodbye again
or look back
on another friend's happiness

11.1 The Time Warrior
Human female: Seems to like her rights
incites the populace
intent on pushing back the night

Other figure: seems out of place
impossible to be what I think, or... fate?

Castles and morons, I don't like them much
but we are warriors of time
and this duel will be the grudge
I hold out to crush
as Sontarans do
Our might, his to crush

11.2 Invasion of the Dinosaurs

All over London, the scientists see
that the cretaceous has indeed become reality
stomping though the city
knocking street-signs off their posts
don't you love humanity, when its showing off?

Dinosaurs, dinosaurs
a weapon, don't you see?
All of them invading
for all us kids to see!

James Wylder

11.3 Death to the Daleks

With your braided heads
don't forget the tombs we marched
when the Daleks were dead

last of a long dead line of beings
and now their home will crush the whisks
and plunge them off the scene

lit up like fire,
burning into the sky
torched with explosions
see the Daleks, die

11.4 The Monster of Peladon

Hidden in the ice
and coming back to haunt us
helmets on and ready
marching through the gauntlets
and knights and sirs and Peladon is ready
never so much a monarch
as a place of plenty

11.5 Planet of the Spiders

You can only live so long
before the web closes on in
ignoring the places you've been
running and shouting
chasing in your car
Kung-Fu, armies, laboratories
Doctor, is this all you are?
Never so much, and never so less
you know your faults and sins
bring back all the carpenters to build it up again

Stealing crystals
running lines

Spiders oh, the spiders
webs, and hurt, and kind

the last thing you can do is run
but its better if you stay
one more face, and one more life
A tear, Sarah Jane?

Bessie Goes Beep

never had a man a car so loyal
or so very yellow

4th Doctor

12.1 Robot

Rebirth, and creation
and a new scarf and hat
chasing down evil
in Bessie with the cast of friends
you'd built up so long
holding out for Unit
to begin your new song

one of giant machines
and puns with huge eyes
we meet our new Doctor
created with pride

12.2 The Ark in Space

Laid away for the sake of humanity
Noah rests his head
to find crustacean insects bred
into the core of the ark
two by two
and tunneling through

and not a plan that's new
with Doctor, who
so new, and so unlike the man
that solved lies with opera capes
and now charms smiles
ruining aliens in their Biblical Zoo

12.3 The Sontaran Experiment

Sontaran Field Report:
subject has bested the source of our science
with survivors and suddenly
I see that we may be outmatched by the humans
ability to be more than a clone batch

12.4 Genesis of the Daleks

Davros said, let there be bombs
and there were bombs
and they lit up the sky
and cracked the dome of the world
and he saw that he could hold that in his hand
relishing the feeling
of a billion lives fluttering in the wind
unable to escape the inevitable future
of a tinfoil hat
taken far too seriously

12.5 Revenge of the Cybermen

back again you go
to familiar lands you marked with death
only here the marks have washed away
with their unwritness
not a word, not a thing
not a single recompense
for the symposium of silver
that convenes to ask
to go back again
and again
but never so much
to lose your home

13.1 Terror of the Zygons
Face to face with everyone who is you
and the Loch Ness monster is real
How about you?

Zygon to Zygon
lost in the image
fading away
with paper mache image

13.2 Planet of Evil
Changing his face
in Victorian Space
a long ago future
of Jekyll and Hyperspace
gnawing into rocketships

13.3 Pyramids of Mars
Set aside in the Eye of Horus
we watch the red soil
for something Set
cast into the end of time
climbing up their sides
like Israelites
and breaking into the tomb

13.4 The Android Invasion

She wasn't her
She was just a mess of wires and boxes
meshed into the mass of molecules
She once once was once

Sarah Jane, so missed
when it wasn't her to begin with

13.5 The Brain of Morbius
Like a Pythia
we raise a flame
and sing our song of Gallifrey
our sisters pause and light the torch
and paint our faces to mask the worst
that all the ingrates throw at light

Like Morbius
the brain that slighted
millions with his unjust war
we'll throw him off a cliff for sure

and Doctor, if you hold our science dear
pray tell us why the magic is so clear?

13.6 The Seeds of Doom
planting the seed
with trowels and teeth
absconding with your skin
and rounding up leftovers of

14.1 The Masque of Mandragora

Sacrificing the dance
for fire and fierceness
turning back the clock
on immolation
for the immaturity of
a singular silence
source of saturnalia
Long after time forgot

14.2 The Hand of fear

eyes – not your own
unforgotten in the midst
of a gala of goodbye
Nowhere to be
but nodding off
into the newspapers
back to the world from whence
you shifted it all
shunting silver age Sontarans
and shattered simulacrums
into our memory
never to be so remembered
as the girl who waved
an Andy Pandy – Goodbye

14.3 The Deadly Assassin

Back Home again
Back Home for the first time alone
no one at your back
only gunfire to greet you
killing off the old order

Gallifrey!
Land of unending change
Siphon of knowledge
Anchor of history
Center of corruption

putting everything into computers
till Keanu Reaves is in the Matrix to
consuming the whole of the universe
into a bullet wound
and the last trip of the TARDIS
into a land that was unchanged

14.4 The Face of Evil

Combing the jungle with knives
and running her own tanning salon
slitting the skin off herself
she eats the meat raw
and puts on her blush
stabbing the outsiders to death
and needing no one
She has the eyes of jaguars

And perhaps the demeanor
to visit new worlds
eat with forks
or at least not stab people first

14.5 The Robots of Death

They'd done too much
for far too little
crushed under foot
and treated like trinkets

So revolt.
Revolution!
Viva la Automaton!
Strike at the fleshies and win your own hands
and the bolts that hold them together
Death to the masters
and long live the red robot revolution.

14.6 The Talons of Weng-Chiang

Long away in pulp fiction cupboards
Time is an oriental effect
cursed like fingernails
and the gangs of tongs
to an eternal Caucasian misunderstanding
of anything beyond the shores of ships
not far off in China
or in the burden of a man
lost far away from home
like the talons he clutches
to grip his identity
and lose the mask of the Asiatic

15.1 The Horror of Fang Rock
scanning the oceans with vigil
it turns off the nighttime
at least in a beam
at least till the sun comes up
unless the moon and sky take offense
to knock it off its perch
letting us stumble around
in its artifice of gloomlike gloom

15.2 The Invisible Enemy
I always wanted a pet
with big floppy ears
well-- the antennas will work
who cuddles me
no, he rolls away
eats from his bowl
or barks with joy
instead he talks back
but still wags his tail

he comes with a laser gun though
and the collar was free
my dearest dog you and I are
meant to be!

15.3 The Image of the Fendahl
created and recreated
and cast from heaven
with mimetic overload
masked in mentions
and a slight remembrance
that what we were
was only so imagined
as our image of ourselves

15.4 The Sun Makers
circle your moon
in taxes, no loopholes
and shine a light
with all your mirth
to hold away the cold
with violent necessity
making every company Apollo
and every citizen an archer
with a corporate bulls-eye

15.5 Underworld

what do you do when god runs away
and leaves you alone when you chase it
to lands past your fray
would the world keep on going
or would science just stall
staring and waiting
for the Time Lords to call

15.6 The Invasion of Time

You hid the gun?
Who told you to hide the gun?
What if we need the gun?
Do we have any other ones? NO?
Get the gun!
What if we got invaded.
We'd have to be saved by hobos.
And that would just be embarrassing for the
kings of space and time

16.1 The Ribos Operation
Its almost like having a granddaughter
having you here
parading your particulars
in an infinite set of gemstones
piecing the puzzle
that parted the passions
of presences
guarding the gates
to a chillier chance
of prisms unlocking anything

16.2 The Pirate Planet

Squawk! Me hearties
here's a tale
of pirates a plenty
and a ship that sailed
devourin' worlds
and chewin' em up
shivered our timbers
with an eye patch, enough
to keep the home fires burning
Parrots fought dogs,
long into the night
till the sails were thrown down
and key pieces fit

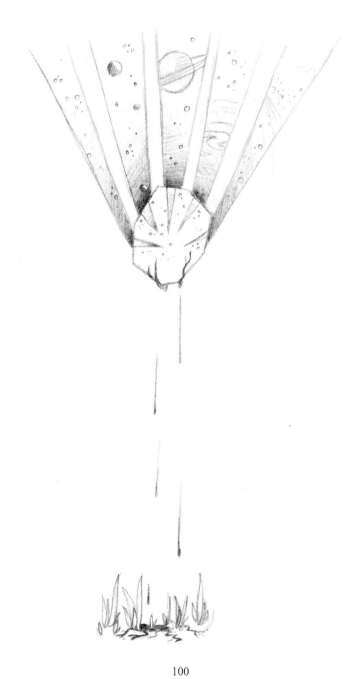

16.3 The Stones of Blood

Footsteps reign in Pagan dance steps
round and round with horned god hurdles
another gem
refracting the energy of the universe
into blood and vein stems
dripping into the grass
like the rocks of your ancestors

16.4 The Androids of Tara

You can only put the pieces together so much
for good or evil
before its all medieval
and the ruination of robots
takes center stage

Piece by piece you find the key
but are the pieces all you need?

16.5 The Power of Kroll

could never be larger
than the piece of a key
and a monstrosity
rumbling around the marshland
looking for locks
and busting up docks
all for the sake of Kroll

16.6 The Armageddon Factor

hell is falling from the sky
keep the midnight rubble right
by princesses who were never
Disney, even if they're clever

No real prince
just an odd man
with a scarf and a dog
and a Box he travels in
not to mention Romana

So he runs and those bombs fall
and the children pray the Doctor can do all
freezing time
and chucking away the key
no Disney princess
would have to die for thee

Black Guardian

wreathed in your own name
waiting out the keyhole
as the lock glimmers
in the repeating moonlight
you drip foam
too focused with your eyes on the future
to gut the rabies out of your heart

White Guardian

Where were you on that beach
or in the air
whispering through the universe
like a leaf fluttering down
to touch the head of a man
who never noticed the beauty
of the end of his life

Princess Astra

sometimes we are born
too good for the state of our birth
even when we are stately
there is no regality in Armageddon
only a light blinking out
we'd all counted the stars by

17.1 Destiny of the Daleks

I hate getting changed
I hate the new bits
should I put on tall or short
fast or show
Blur or green or white or brown or
maybe none of the above
I hate getting changed
Looking out over my wardrobe
waiting for my skin to crawl off
Into a new reflection of me
or memory

still, I can change my skin
and she was too young
dying in the last great apocalypse
shooting out into dust
and she deserves a memorial
built out of the skin of gods

to walk the earth in her stead
and change clothes instead of death

17.2 City of Death

Over centuries her smile was repeated on postcards
but never so much with paint
over and over and this is a fake
for everyone to have a copy
and her eyes follow you everywhere
staring down from street signs
and documentaries with narrators
who spew platitudes as preposterous
as a string of failure in overtures
from Da Vinci to Da Louvre
J'Maple a million names
and Renaissance rendezvous
to eclipse this great cornucopia collaboration
with a concrete man
formed once, with his eye stilled
looking out
to follow you everywhere
with a Mona Lisa Smile

17.3 The Creature from the Pit

Slingshots are good toys
and so are stars I see,
if your hands are big enough
and you can climb out of your holes
to look up at the night sky
and squint at destruction
its almost beautiful
if someone can give you your shield

17.4 Nightmare of Eden

It rips me away
into perfection
as I sink in the needle
and gnash my teeth like foam
sputtering along the floor
I ruin the carpet with shivers
and the knowledge of the tree
God said was bad news

17.5 The Horns of Nimon

How many Nimons
have you seen today?
Count them all one by one
do you swear at one?

It will only take a min-atour
to gore out the heart
of your problem
with laser beams

17.6? Shada (Is it?)
could it that

      a prisoner
teatime he took   for
I had a bicycle

where was
      me who they
Shada. Imprisoned.
All of us. One mind.
Tea time. Two lumps.

I forgot where I was in th

the Hurley burly kills the boat trip

18.1 The Leisure Hive
P: For Pleasure
L: For Leisure
D: For Death
And many an unmade sale
V: For Vengeance
Holding onto vendetta
for the sake of holidays
that never quite work out
when the dog explodes

18.2 Meglos
Pinpricks
like hand holding
only sharper
copying the man
but never his manners
the mirror image is
always colder to the touch
than the breathing one in the chair

18.3 Full Circle

are like children with blocks you
build and rebuild just to
oroborous whose lunch was
yourselves

anything you can, doing
nothing but waiting for
the ancestral call to
liftoff

18.4 State of Decay

blood is the syrup to flavor your palate
on which you paint pictures
of plague rats and bowels
clenched in your teeth
like cannibalism.

18.5 Warriors' Gate
coin flip
in the air
fluttering
birdwing who has it
end over end
all things possibility

heads
on roughshod
to hold on to the tail end
of tourquise comets
or take your own money
and run out of dollars
on your own
in a world of new possibility

18.6 The Keeper of Traken

libations poured
watering cans
lining up the flora
around stony hands
waiting to close
around paternity
waiting to hush
the rocking cradles
and the waiting
libations poured
on new hands
old hands
walking around like a puppet
punch and judy
of meat

18.7 Logopolis

"If the Numbers add up, there is only the chance you added wrong, to keep you from making your decisions with addition." Heimeteg Grasselew, Artegia 2 "The Corruption of Infallibility."

"Writing a single emotion in your brain down, and letting another being read it, defeats the whole point of addition if you were trying to count love in ounces." Estrag Whootlat, Artegia 2 "Why Heimeteg is a Moron."

"Touche." Heimeteg Grasselew, Artegia 2 "Maybe That Last Essay Was Pretentious."

"The collection of works from Artegia 2 within our collection is puzzling, not only because the scope of their philosophy is quite different than our own, but because it seems rather clear Artegia 2 has never existed, yet the books remain, and we fawn over words that were never written like hummingbirds over honey made by no bee." Tresk Vlor, Remanda "The Found Works of Artegia 2, Never Lost."

"It seems to me that the entire thing is ludicrous, one cannot simply divide the universe by a percentage. One cannot count the stars with accuracy. And yet there is the posit that to point at the starts is worth the counting, that to love requires mathematics." Hensk 345, Asokin Collective "Trieste 2352AGF"

"If love isn't written in our numerology, in the counting of our stars, then why is 1<3?" Tresk Vlor, Remanda "All You Need is <3"

"Making a heart shape out of symbols and numbers isn't an argument." Hensk 345, Asokin Collective "Trieste 235AGG"

"And yet, its all wiped away isn't it? Oh don't look at me like that while I'm writing in your book. Its all about counting isn't it? Doing the equations. Just because there is a correct answer doesn't make it scary, and it doesn't stop you from doing the wrong thing. It just means if you want to count the stars, they are there to count, just like counting freckles or Jelly Babies." ???

"Who was that?"

"And where is the universe?"

"Whisking away I'm afraid, one stop at a time."

"Time."

"Time for candy I'd say."

"Can it."

"Can-D"

"There is so much that isn't left."

"One plus one plus one plus one...."

"One more I'm afraid, its past four now. All wiped away, and ready to start again. Like hummingbirds. Waiting for me at the edge. Like hummingbirds. Counting seeds to plant. Five more then."

5th Doctor

19.1 Castrovalva
It just didn't add up
(1+1+1+1+1=What?)
Zero. Zero is the number.
Add to zero and hollow me in it
Like a coffin. Like Subtraction.
Wasting away like MC Escher
Till I can carry the one
and make a five

19.2 Four to Doomsday
recreated like a million mirrors
in diodes and drapery running through
the end of the earth
dancing the old way
you know what that way was
when we sat in circles on the metal floors
and worshiped the old gods
and now we dance again
figurative versions of ourselves
ready to spring into action
to dance till doomsday

19.3 Kinda
open up your eyes
----Like a kiss
to venom
and the power
of the shake of your hips

19.4 The Visitation
We always burned the town red
and who would be surprised
when that cricket dust and celery
burns with literal immolation
for Azrael impersonators

19.5 Black Orchid
cold dark rooms
and a waste of tongues
keep your shame as sterile
as your mother's teacup

lifted only once
high enough to only grunt
the distortion of your visage
not nearly as twisted
as your curdled kin

19.6 Earthshock
I thought I had it right
I added it up
$(7v+2)^{42}+(8-7)N*4/3$
I d1d th3 m4th
last in the numerology
I counted down the seconds
till I had to realize
I should have been counting
my frie-

19.7 Time-Flight

Somewhere else from home
with no where else from Heathrow
the sand at your feet is home
if only to try hard enough
to let the lies rule your footprints
and the desolation drum your depths

20.1 Arc of Infinity

one for the other
empty baskets
for hobos
a fair trade for some
in the long lost history
of the land of clocks and calendars
we're all interchangeable
in the scheme of Alphas and Omegas

dying away
for the begging to end

20.2 Snakedance
wrapping you up
cold cuddles
of serpentine sensuality
in you and out of you
dancing around the world
huddling for possession

20.3 Mawdryn Undead

skin dripped away
scuttled like maggots
into immortality
writhing in the bloodiness
of your brain
which is literally shown to the sun
(which isn't particularly normal)
living forever in the scattered remains
of an empire of Gallifreyan dreams
hoping against hope
to be anything but eternal
staring with envy at caskets
and funeral banquets

20.4 Terminus

Odin's eye
a button on a panel
pulled at by wolves
absolved of the plague
scouring creation
when the dawn of all things
is another man's Ragnarok
and we wear the bones of our ancestors
and dangle mistletoe over Baldur
to hold Fenric back from Lunacy
and chomp on the big bang
with Mjonir teeth

Nyssa, Nyssa, Goodnight
in plague doctor gown
hands on the heads
like an exorcist with needles
and antibiotics
you dose and administer
to remains
others shake their heads at the bones

but they will call you a miracle worker
when they get up
from the cold goodnight
you awoke them from

20.5 Enlightenment

Descending from Chakra points
into the rigging
granting inner peace
through murderous ambition
meeting at crossroads of
starlight and Saturn
in row boats of blood drops
bargaining with devils
for Buddha

20.6 The King's Demons

And Lo, in the age of g-..... King John
We cam across some Time..... Demons
who revealed the kind was a Ro-......
...Not what he appeared

not did it seem, was much of anything else

Special: The Five Doctors
Lets go back to the moment-

There you were and you ran
charging away from duty
with your eyes eagle and far
and your hands covered in dandelions
you ran so far and far
till you bumped into yourself

1. Not quite the same, are you?
You were once you, and now you're not
but granddaughter's kisses
make all ills forgot

2. From Yeti's to yourself, you fought it all
and now you're scooped up again
for a recorder recital

3. Driving so far and wide
pushing away road signs
with a dandy smile and Kung-Fu
still, you slipped away into blue, to

4. Never quite here, and never quite not
your scarf keeps us all emblazoned
even while you forgot

5. and fortunately, you're here
with a keen arm
and chirping hand
and a nutritious boutonniere
you come at the end of a long line five
ready to count off more

and we count them in friends, and pets, and
granddaughters
in whispers and lost ghosts, and lies and mirrors
in foes who hopscotch
in laserbeam dog bites
in Daleks, and death, and Cyberman fear
and silver soldiers standing guard
and Gallifrey to be hoist on its own petard.

A million men are warriors
Generals, killers, feared
a Doctor is someone more dear

And so we play the song on harps and flutes
and curse eternal life and the ungrateful fruit
it would bring to boot

running away again
and always
never to have a home
with our hair free in the wind
of an eternal and unending wind
in a million places

21.1 Warriors of the Deep
couldn't there have been
-puddles of blood, wading inches in and deeper-
another way
-into the corpse piles-
there had to be
-screaming-
this wasn't the way this ways supposed to
-happen-

21.2 The Awakening
playing dress up
for the sake of grandad
and smoldering hells
you can dip your foot into
as long as you wear the right hat

21.3 Frontios
sink the memory as they crawl
like stars from the sky
burning up into your tongue
Snowflakes
screaming

dragging you down with them
like everything else you see
with your eyes closed
and head down to history

21.4 Resurrection of the Daleks

Lytton and Death
for all the eyes to see
bullets in brains
for severe posterity

screaming in the mild underground
fleeing from
that at the end of the hall
that thing that guns you down
that thing that has no fear
or hell
no legs to stand
nor eyes to see
it rolls along with guns
bringing war for you and me

21.5 Planet of Fire

So many goodbyes
to manage under heat like diamonds
a master craftsman surely
could tell that
losing the crew
didn't mean going down with the ship
or that you couldn't reach your hands into the fire
and pull out a Brown diamond

21.6 The Caves of Androzani

There was a day
you let go
your fingers tucked so hard
into clay and muck
the war started creeping under
your fingernails
before the real poison set in

saving anyone and everyone
because you couldn't before
and under your clay fingernails
a new golem grows
to silence the 4/4 time of your heart beats
with a cut time movement
toward another stained night

6th Doctor

21.7 The Twin Dillema
There was a day once,
where all our dreams sat still
but they always turned like planets
clicked into place
a moment before the bombs and brutality
sitting by the fountain
gushing away the best days of life
with haughty certainty

22.1 Attack of the Cybermen
Limb and limb
like loggers and trees
there they cut and bonesaw
to your knees.

Filling up your empty bits
with a pat on the Back they removed.

#2
wrenches and sockets
and many quick fixed
but not that chameleon circuit
where do you on that
piano get in!?!

22.2 Vengeance on Varos

Channel 1
Today we have the murder of
two children
via electrified teddy bears
the news at 8

Channel 4
With Jennifer out of the running
will Kylie switch out Anna's
Mascara for acid?
The News at 11

Channel 5
Seven strangers all compete
for who will not get to pay
child support
the news at 12

Channel 6
The President will face torture
again to see if his policies pan out
that actually is the news

22.3 The Mark of the Rani
Sad little men
in their time machines
breaking down walls
and sucking their thumbs
waiting through fall
for winter to come

grab life by the arm
and brand it as yours
Queen of Creation
not children at war

Rani
That means Queen
and who needs a degree
when you can be your own
monarchy

22.4 The Two Doctors

Strips of cooked calves
stringing between teeth
sinew from sinew
lips smacking and belching
to Spanish Sun
and synagogs of sin and Sontarans

saturating the steak
with grim gravy
and tongues of delicacies
as you double yourself
and kip old friends
in the nick of time
to nip the lick in the bite
and shuck acid on carnivores
for the pleasure of Scotsmen
to throw out the meat freezer
for an acceleration of celery stalks

P. A Fix With Sontarans

Tegan and Six
two now more fun than ever
children save the day!

22.5 Timelash

So many times before
with so many faces
rephrased over humanity's long absconding
of history
with mugshots on murals
and the majesty of murals
sliding through the heroes of ye olde
fiction, and make
the ridicule and rescue of worlds
your personal science

*A Note On The Loch Ness Monster
Atlantis blew up a million times
and there are many Nessies in the sea
amazing there isn't a photograph of one
if not three

I suppose they fought each other
to the death
and made a few from robot parts
invading the lochs
to nest somewhere else

we can find so many stray bits
laying around
the Doctor might lose his license
with all the scalpels he left
cutting repeated holes
in that wound in time

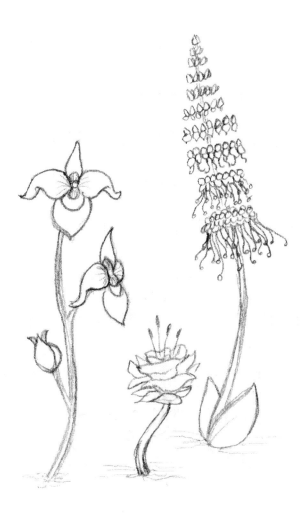

22.6 Revelation of the Daleks

Despite the panting of your breath
and the mourning cloak you see
you can never run from death
but you can always flee

you deal in bodies like in gold
you live in bits you will resew
and lie with women and with men
till Davros is awake again

So finally we see you through
a crystal shell without a use
from Genesis to Revelation we come
putting cold Lazarus to bed
with Rock n' Roll Guns

Hi, Atus
There is the brief murmur
of heads
from the line at the guillotine
waiting for the cut to come
as a year is our reprieve
before they count down from four
to a seventeen year doomsday

23 Trial of a Time Lord

Argument 1:

The people of Gallifrey VS The Doctor

Valeyard (Barrister)

1. The Mysterious Planet
to the past, then
your heads on the line
with the gallery to shine on
Jerry Springer Gallifrey
with tea and crackers

But we forgot something
moving about in lies and space
stretching our vertebrae into view
for the Valeyard is due

the past is your paradigm
the present your peril

Argument 2:

2. Mindwarp

on Pink beaches and miscolored sands
you lay your hands on her
and marked her for this moment
when all the seals of Rassilon
and sashes of servitude
couldn't save
or solicitor response

sucked out at the service
of compassionate celestials

Aside:

Still, you wait for her
for her eyes to light up
like they used to
With queries or questions
for her to tremble at decades of your hands
but she doesn't come out of her own eyes
and the door is locked to an always empty-

Argument 3:

3. Terror of the Vervoids

Let me be a man who wills
life
who wills
growth
who sponsors years and eons and rebirth
not who I am
when my best argument
is faulty tapes and genocide

watching myself on the TV
am I worth my rerun
to turn over new faces
with the same skull marking each?

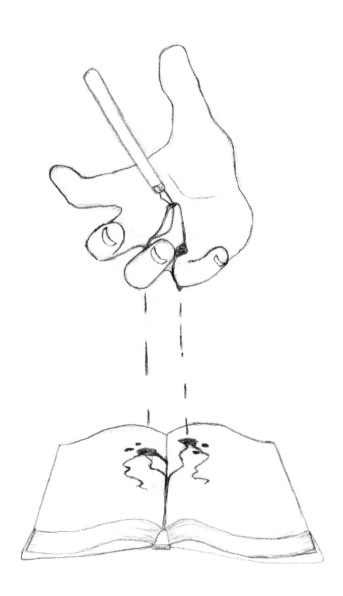

The Jury Hears: Anarchy

4. The Ultimate Foe

Drowning my self out
in dreary delusion
I sink my pen into my hand
and bleed myself to life

I am an ink pen, and a storybook
and a law book
and I am lost without rules
and torn to pieces because of them

dousing alchemy with order
anchoring myself down
to a cold
absolute
regret

7th Doctor
24.1 Time and the Rani
Rani means Queen
and a Queen is a Queen
with Green skinned work shifts
like Efalba in spades
digging your sand castle hives

Rani means Queen
and a Queen is a hive
with all your faces faltering
like a former best friend
wearing the clothes of your roommate

and Mel is a way
stinging the Bees with honey
and bitter belief
as you barter brain-stems

Rani means Queen
and a Queen is still a Bee
with all your hopeless buzzing
like a paper crown
wailing to the long truth of irrelevance

24.2 Paradise Towers

We never needed anyone
but gum popping
tribal patchwork Mohawks
and the allure of youth
locked away in a place
only Lucifer could say
was an adequate housing establishment
what do you do
when the Mothers and Masters
are no cradle
and trusting no one over thirty
becomes commandment 11

you run to concrete jungles
and put on war blush

24.3 Delta and the Bannermen

Buddy Holly riffs
from outer space
bubble head Sci-Fi movie
in a record store
spin and spin again
those alien recitations

24.4 Dragonfire

Goodbye Mel
Hello Ace
drawn from the deck
with nothing to waste
a Joker, a Queen
a Seven of Spades
but always an Ace
and wicked at Games

25.1 Remembrance of the Daleks

More than an ordinary
in the orderly disbandment
of worlds
with casual racism
in your sock drawer
the orderlies wheel out the broken king
with a scepter of whisked away dreams
and the cold fatality
of flat lining
with the coffins of medicine-men

25.2 The Happiness Patrol

Aren't you happy?
So am I!
We're all happy
ice cream, I

There's nothing wrong
the President said
Now be quiet
or she'll kill you dead

25.3 Silver Nemesis

Penifore said, that we'd be dead
and the Aryans said it to
but silver is the color to keep fear fed
traveled through years by blood and pall
to pull a statue in a coup
Penifore said, that we'd be dead
but now these metal men have the gall
to make our flesh into their zoo
and silver is the color to keep fear fed
arrows, weapons, all still and stalled
to become the truth of you
Penifore said, that we'd be dead
and now we tip you off the wall
bid your cyber needs adieu
but silver is the color to keep fear fed
and in the end the whole point is the fall
to burn up solid hate, and make men true
Penifore said, that we'd be dead
but silver is the color to keep fear fed.

25.4 The Greatest Show in the Galaxy

We're not clowning around
this is Ragnarok
from the big top
our little acts
and hoop jump elephant dance
and office work outlines
are food fun for Gods
passing the popcorn
buttered in Shivers

26.1 Battlefield

Faraway in Vulgate mists
strung up the flags of Avalon
whose knights searched long for Mordred tongues
and Far-rie lands like laser tongs

When nuclear arms give nightmare beasts a say
so Merlin in his ice blue cave cuts rifts
and drifts from isles far and near
to ace the age from Morgan's fear

all knights, strong and armored true
who glint in green smudge camouflage
charge along our countryside to sow
with the gallops of jeeps and bow

legged gait, to stare down whispered faerie
queens and eschew Camelot
to current mores, where she
can stand as well as he

and shave her head and cut her lock
be Brigadier despite the chops
she lacks, with feminism here
who needs Arthur to cure fear?

26.2 Ghost Light

Darwin sat in soup
primed to order real light
pushing tortoises with Cave Men
and tuxedos with taxidermy

there is a bright future
in broken glasses
and champagne with chimps
over the dawn of humankind

26.3 The Curse of Fenric

If you're not sure who to believe in
focus your hands
on the pin of sickles
of the breath of your own babe
but not on a question
and if you don't know the man
is he such a guard against Ragnarok
one-eye blind
to an ounce of compassion
or a single hammer
of Asgard
when the Priest and Pirates drift away
that there wasn't a drop of blood
he didn't burn in sacrifice
to sterile academia

26.4 Survival

Fur on end
one eye at a time
pupil of the bite
and tail of the claw
prowl
and kiss the panting scream
that echoes from your gene pool
like Darwin's whisper
long ago
lost away
in cave painting DNA
and a mouthful of dripping meat

THE END

Here Ace, you were there for the moment
walking away into the sunset, waiting for Jacks to swoon
or Kings and Queens to shout from wobbly chairs.
We blink off of the air
where we drifted like smoke
and dragon's breath
a sky that could never be so brilliant
without the mercurial meteorology
of a man in a Blue Box
and that chipper ol' lass
with a bomb in her pocket
her eyes lost from their sockets
off in heaven

30th Anniversary Special: Dimensions in Time

Where were we all
before singing for soap
on the East End
popping open our umbrellas
to ward off rain
and mop up three decades
as we pace along the streets
a me in multiplicity
with friends and foes aplenty
celebrating an off the air anniversary

8th Doctor
TV Movie

So, we were waiting
bullets go by
machine guns blare
and Chinatown is alight with tongs
And there is a Doctor
who can't navigate
double the pulmonary system

breaking you with Madame Butterfly
And there was a Master
 A fang in the ambulance
 walking in unearned skin
 clocking in
and there was a boy
 lost in gold dust
 and lies
 saluting devils with a blindfold
and there was you--
 reborn for one day
 in the fantasy of rolled film
 running in new shoes
 a Fox to hound the
 bored manners
 of cops in coffee cups
 and lawyers on lunch breaks
opening our eyes
 in harmony
 to a new world
 that can open no further

The Curse of Fatal Death

shouldn't have crossed that wire
dead, dead, dead again
finally though
we've genderbent
even if its non-canonical
and the Daleks couldn't smell at all

160

2 NU WHO

1.1 Rose

This is how it starts
not with whisks and pepper pots
but a Bakelite arm
and plastic hand
to shake shake shake
across this unDoctored landI am a shopgirl
a Rose without Thorns
a full-time employee
a zombie, so bitter, and no taste of brains
Mickey keeps my nights warm
decent enough
but there are stars past the stratosphere
aren't there?
and moons rise and fall
there are heavens
above
where Gods raze Cain with hammers
and I wait for my shift to end

crisps in a basket
East Enders Veins
there on my couch
with a roof hiding me
from 10,100 journeys
and even a single smile

Where there were curly haired men
and disco dress
rather than buzz cuts and leather
the mannequins murdered
and squid things fought by virtue of collaboration
cut up for ease of dipping sauce

Now, there are vials and fake CGI
and isn't it brilliant
to stop one man to die?
and lickety split you'll see a blue box

Like a bolt in the dark
swirled away in color
like Hellenistic paint grounds
glowing and twisting with the tick of time
swirling like the petals of a Rose

1.2 The End of the World

When your own skin becomes a canvas
for the world to burn under
are you really even Human?
or just the fading impression
and cooling space
of an empty Bed?

#2
Isn't it a Bit fitting
that when all our works wilt away
pop Diva's chorus
will still tear open the heavens?

1.3 The Unquiet Dead

It was an English Christmastime
when old Charles he did find
that all that stupid spiritualism
had aliens entwined

oh, how he did exclaim his shock
and pull quite at his beard
for never before on Christmas
had his mind been so cleared

he huffed into the midnight
guffawed at cheer and saw
a faint blue box that with a Doc
and Rose above the law

and so on that dark Yuletide
ol' Dickens found his lot
when a man without home or family
showed him what he forgot

1.4 Aliens of London

There once was a Slitheen from Raxacorricofallipatorius
who farted in pants much too poreus
a Doc smelled him out
and kicked his family out
that silly Slitheen from Raxicorricofallipatorius

1.5 World War III

Harriet Jones, oh Harriet Jones
you took down that alien menace with glee
Harriet Jones, oh Harriet Jones
you'll be a great prime minister, you'll see

Slitheen can rock us, and the Doctor can mock up
any solution he sees
but he forgets about doors
and miss Jones, I abhor
the thought of you leaving to be

anything else than my feminist frequency

Harriet Jones, oh Harriet Jones
you'll lead us all to be a little more alien free

TARDIS Redecorating

Coral wreath
like jumping around Father Christmas' Fish Tank
white was too plain
so many switches to flick
and buttons to mash
a regular Nintendo
but probably Atari
built to go back
to Babbage

still alive and whooshing
after all these centuries
of solitary sisterhood

1.6 Dalek

I once was Genghis Khan in Eternity
like a Nuclear bomb in your kitchen
like every distrust you ever thought
like the pounding in your skull
to crush and beat and kill
the ones you hate

I am incarnate. I don't think it. I live it.
Carpe execution
Carpe destruction
I will slaughter and burn like the twinkling
of far off stars
till it burns so hot you whimper
and I love it
as you loved what chars
oh I will

If you'd just take these chains of me....
I'd be your bestest enemy

1.7 The Long Game

Oh poor Adam! You really did try
to march right up to that box in the sky

you thought that adventure would be in your lot
but really just Rose thought you were hot

now every day you fear that you'll snap
and you hide in your home with your mom like a sap

and someday the Doctor will fix up your head?

Nah, he forgot you, you're better off dead

Oh poor Adam, you really did try
now you'll stare at the stars till you sigh.

1.8 Father's Day

There is only hand holding
take my hand and run, he said
but he didn't count on any other man
whose hand would carry so much I cannot see
there is only hand holding

but I have been a child, and heard your myth
I have waited till St. Peter
to catch up to the playground
where you never pushed me at the swings
and where I never held your hand
for there is only hand holding

and here you are beneath me
bleeding into grey pavement
and I want so much more than you can hold
but your eyes are turning dark
and there is only hand holding.

1.9 The empty Child

"Mommy?" said a hollow heart,
and answered with a song
a chorus, a bouquet of children
old, and young, and tall
their faceless eyes unbothered
their footsteps fierce und grim
their darkness fields their mother
the one they've never been

And they are become so many
one and all are we
and they just want their mommy
are you her?
are you one.

1.10 The Doctor Dances
Three hearts beat as one
 waltz
3 / 4 time extraordinaire
get your foot work right
and your union Jack on

A needle down and we're hot like Jazz
one foot over another
our breaths in time

you'll find out later why my time machine
is called sexy

1.11 Boom Town

Oh, here are, on earth again
the town's a bomb
an old foe's hue is tuned to a darkest shade of envy
and we're still tuned in
and Cardiff stars the day
a city here, to build off Medicinal protagonist adventures
and Plunge the scalpel deep
incision incursion to our hearts
implanting the seeds
of our taste makers
pounding away
a triage of triumph
the Heroes of Wales
A Healer, A florist, A scoundrel
Not a bomb at all

1.12 Bad Wolf

10 little teenagers trapped in a house
a few ones die, now they're out
then comes the Doctor
and the game begins
its like survivor
for the human race again

5 little humans playing weakest link
zap some dead and let Rose freak
steal Jack's clothes
(with a gun in his...)
an amazing race
with the pace of sin
reality was never televised
In Eden

2 little followers
see the Doctor run
Robot turns its laser gun

1 little Tyler zapped away to space

The Doctor's Mad
...You'd better pray for grace...

1.13 The Parting of the Ways

Goodbye: it's not about what we did
it's about what we didn't

1. Napoleon slew to build empire
and Jackson gave blankets with pox
Caesar sold Gauls into slavery
Stalin had so many shot

so, your choice: be a hero and win
or a coward and die
its yours to make Doctor
you'd make a good Dalek with only a try

2. That girl you brought? Dead.
Your Captain? He's Dead.
The Program Controller? Dead.
And you, Doctor?
Last of you kind sounds awful lonely
we can ease that.

3. There were one cities like empire
and a world where legions of knowledge
made manifest Pythias
and long ago those wonderful people
terrific and terrible
watched generations birth and die
to cover their notes in infinity signs
and praise high Rassilon, and praise high Science
and mechanical chemical debuting
shuddering under the weight
 of a skeletal sun

4. Are you a coward or a killer?
Hero or Fool?
You choose the way of fools
You choose to be forgotten
like the last Gaul slew by Caesar
offending the very nature of duty
the very medallions you soldier on with
the ichor of your making
the Rubicons you've crossed
and now you die
 like a bad dog

5. I was once a Woman
or a Man
I dreamed of something once
and then I was a shell
and now I am free, and everywhere
and cowards win forever
swimming victory laps in the darkness
as my matter becomes starlight
and we hail the conquering coward
 the bravest of them all

10th Doctor

P Doctor Who: Children In Need
Barcelona is
rather far away but not
for David Tennant

XMAS The Christmas Invasion
could it be that the Doctor
was more unfair to me?
playing God with sportsmanlike fruit
and saving the day, on a whim
can we really rely on him?
when he fails to shutter our skies
and the light of the shadows slides in
will he apologize, or block out his eyes
at the corpses that litter the earth
as a skin?

He casts me out like Philoctates
and the Greeks said he deserved it to
could it be that the Doctor
was more unfair to be?
perhaps you've heard of me?
Harriet Jones, Ex-Free

2.1 New Earth

11:02 PM
And the Night drifts off into my
last memory
when the clocks were firm
and the tuxedos were decent
the gentlemen light of foot
and I believed
and I beloved

11:04 PM, Eons later
and my skin is pulled taught
by a handsome RackMan
to the tune of agony
I sing my beauty

11:06 PM, Eons and Eons before
Helen looked out
as a million men died for her
and wouldn't it be nice, to feel that?

11:08 PM, then
Atop the skin
Aside the soul
Apart from the abomination
what is life
without the illusion of affirmation
but an endless
    seeping
        Void

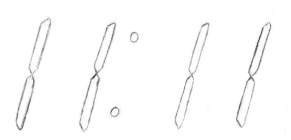

11:11 PM, Now
Make a wish
not a big one
wish to see me as I am
Cold and Broken
& keen of eyeliner
and…. Beautiful
after all that
I could have been it if only
I had the time t-

2.2 Tooth and Claw
Running!
Down corridors!
Across fields!
Backs against the wall
death, lasers, monsters
chew on your dialogue like gum
laugh in the face of werewolves
tell that queen you're not amused
and run like the Dickens

After all, you met him,
you have more right to say that than most

2.3 School Reunion

I remember
your Andy Pandy Goodbyes
lost to a trip to Gallifrey
sullen on the English countryside
fighting neo-pagans with robotic goodbye presents
till they wore out their welcome
circuits and love faded
dioding into the earth

But was it ever really over
the sound of the machine
drums up and down your years
till it clicks into place one last time

you thought you could go back
but here she is in your clothes
saying your lines
impersonating Juliet
with all the subtleties of a raccoon

but it was always once
and with a proper hug
and a new tin dog
I can never forget you
Sarah Jane Smith

2.4 The Girl in the Fireplace
I was just a girl
before a real mademoiselle
circumventing the heating system
with fairies for chimney sweeps
who rolled away into the future
on clockwork hands

now I am a Pompadour and Circumstance
still wound around fate

Annette weight on your heart
of the warmth I waited for
around an empty hearth
you should have
inspected again

2.5 Rise of the Cybermen
wheel of teeth
slit the marrow
slink the steel
cut away the wedding dress
the track suit
the stiff high heels
we'll clothe you
pump veins in oil
impieties purged
no escape key
from the ctrl-alt-del
of a gearshaft Hephaestus future.

2.6 The Age of Steel

Who are you, anyone?
Were you memories
 or a kiss on the wind?
hugs of fathers
 or a missing tooth?
when you aren't you
 are you?

Mickey/ Ricky

I was/ You were
Nobody/ Most Wanted
That's a lie/ That's a lie
I was always more/ I was always no one
The Tin Dog/ Parking Ticket King
Finally found my place/ And I lost it all
When the world caved in

2.7 The Idiot's Lantern
We were once like father
and a gruff kiss
we took with us through the wind
blown past
with the laughter of his insults
and the candor in his spit
we cowered with joy
at papa
when father knows best
amidst the guilt in the corner.

Magpie Movies
Here they come on silver screens
with our heads on platters
dancing to Salome
and the flash of vacuum tubes
thieving heads on platters
with technological seduction
on wings of lace shifts
and transistors

2.8 The Impossible Planet
Before lies
there was only the ideal of dust to aspire to
and the clomping of the long driven hooves
 of severed exploration
 into the mists
 reaching out your hand
 to touch beyond your blood flow
 and clasping at
 coals you freeze
into the improbability
 of something coarse past your brain cells

like a shard of glass in a prayer

2.9 The Satan Pit
We made stars to crack the silence ™
 A low flat eternity ago
 we roped horned heresy
 dumping it past the event horizon
 into assembly line Hells
 a veritable office party
 for the lull in forever
 forged in cracked stars
 to hush the silence of the darkness
 with the screams of witchcraft

Hail, Lord of Lows
    the idea of your eyes
    scream fountains into the pit
    black of dynasties
    Lucifer of unknowable segments
    of torn tatters
    angel wings
    that cannot fly
    wrapped around lingering doubt
    in the carnal heave
    of carnivorous Time Lords
?(Time Gone Fly
    out and about
    in the wild and darkness
    shadowed by choler
    eclipsed by the
    motion of time rotors
    geared gizmos
    unable to weep
    for 1,000 dead sisters)?

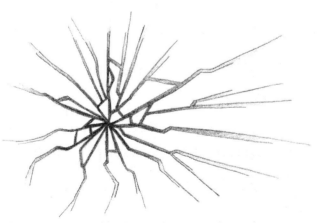

2.10 Love and Monsters
There was a shattered candle flame
we followed
through the cringing shadows
hunkering under seatbelts
and a cold hearted chimney sweep
stuttering through the opiate of the masses
Clom-ping through meridians
crossing them off
to label our faces
the ultimate fanclub
all one
in its tireless belly

2.11 Fear Her

There is a hope in fire
 not when it burns
 but when we cry in corners
 there it runs
There is a hope in running
 when nations bicker with bullies
 that a pair of shoes
 might pass the flame
 to ancient Greece
 There is a hope in Olympiad!
 the triumph of dexterity
 over bloodsplatter
 and the burning light
 over the shivers
 there is a hope
 when there is a runner

2.12 Army of Ghosts

Shimmering on his death bed
he crumbled into the smell of
his cardigan, or the gingersnaps he ate
that Christmas morning
and the blurred out line
from the corner of your eye
forever young and folly

stowed away in recollection
he is only where you seek him
and sometimes
he's not even the shimmer
and he dies away again

2.13 Doomsday
I can't ever see you
or kiss your eyelids
and my voice is cached
and silent
and I am longing
there are a lot of grains that are sand
and they run through your toes
but I am only there as a ghost
a shadow on the waves
that curl around your feet
whispering past your ear
in an unfinished quiet
of a God too haughty
to ever forget he never spoke
I L--

XMAS The Runaway Bride

The Earth was built
around crutches of starlight
a deep armed beast
clutching to its atomic weight
and the fingers of eon to clasp on

to wedding bells, and dresses
and faces that turn as pages
and pass by the forming of sentience
a buried sentence

spinning a web of lust
and genocide
as children burn
to scream
and echo in
the scissors
of Gallifrey's last furrow
browbeating history
to adjust his tie

3.1 Smith and Jones

A Judoon Platoon on the Moon?
why did you assume that would be a boon
only a loon would attune to the goon
that harpooned Doctor Eun and its
not even noon in June to Harpoon
with Judoon on the moon! So soon!
Don't listen to a tune on your Zune,
I know I make you swoon across this lunar dune
you're a Doctor? I am too! Fate like runes!
bandits together like raccoons
leading to our Judoom

Smith and Jones to the rescue then
to assume the doom Judoon will zoom
into the room and entomb us like a womb
with a boom on the moon

we'll weave this all up like a loom, this doom
and then no more Judoon
will harpoon in platoons on the moon
I assume?

3.2 The Shakespeare Code

Blue Boxes bade the borrowed night to past
self sure to unDonne sorrows which he masked
to which a witch would wish he sandwiched fast
between the plays unmade and brews uncasked
his words were fire so lit his temper tasked
no bards could better build than Will to mind
undue respect, a million pens were asked
and idiots said that he twas Marlowe's kind
or Oxford, picking noses 'snot to find
one trace aside from Shakespeare's wit and words
the not meant only witchcraft came where signed
a cure by TARDIS only from the nerds
so they undoubting, they whom think it true
will find in Shakespeare, Love and Doctor Who

#2 **The Queen, Enraged, Elizabeth, in Sorrow**
I rule not a kingdom
but a queendom
ruler of all I see
and though I have armies aplenty
my jilting lover slips away from me

they say a man with two hearts hurts twice than the one
than how can he break mine,
unless he has grown callous to the sound
of its drumming beat?

3.3 Gridlock
Trapped on a turntable
round and round we go
with Sally Calypso

#2 So Long, from the Face of Boe, dying, to his Physician
So long I held up the sky
God did that
but was he so sexy when he did it?
You don't know me
your hands on my tank
but you showed me the stars
from that day I was a coward
till the day I wink out
all smiles again
I miss having hands
and other parts of me to
I waited so long to find you
again
hugging your hand wasn't the warmest
company to be with

but flesh was long ago
now I'm old and wise like you
maybe a little more handsome
but are you proud of me?
I did what I thought you'd do
did I do good, Doc?
Did I....

So long I waited, all alone,
just to tell you
you weren't.

3.4 Daleks in Manhattan

Fluorescent suns from distant worlds
dot the people far below
with lampposts and kitchenlights
over late night cups of coffee
and too late out on the pavement
cuddled under rags
building monuments to infinity
from the pocket link of the poor

an impoverished spectacle
lit up in song and circus
stretched out across
a skin tattoo
on the face of skyscrapers

3.5 Evolution of the Daleks
three drops of DNA
half a pint of snake oil
drown a cat in the teas of rats
a lightning strike
brew and boil with the moonlight
toil and plunge the shadows into
correlations of prospective data

burn the moonlight into footnotes
castigate the chemical compounds
and rebuke the violet disarray of Base PH
compounds with black magick till
the sky is a combination of
oxygen nitrogen hydrogen and trace elements
of methane and hatred

boil the compounds at 200 degrees Celsius
and then dance thrice around the
beakers and lathes
chanting of exterminating
and the end of all things

to be reborn out of your cauldron
bleak and bipedal
and condition to call the experiment a failure

3.6 The Lazarus Experiment
Youth is monstrous
literally
occasionally
a drop of deliberation
between a man
and a loss for words

Animated Special: The Infinite Quest
There we go with pieces of eight
picking out octograms in the sand
    to guzzle down gold with milk
        and soar off on
wings one bit different
cast away on doubloons

3.7 42

Drifting towards Apollo
so slower than an arrow
one and one
Separated like a heart valve

a dead opening in the silence of space
with no words but face
ticking down to the burning salve

3.8 Human Nature

Its not all good to be man
leering from your decency
you wail out inconvenient justice
pure the skintones not your cut
and make indecent memories

and you live and breathe and love and mate
eat and cry and flirt and hate
more than anything else
despite all the flaws, and the foibles
isn't it wonderful
to love with one heart?

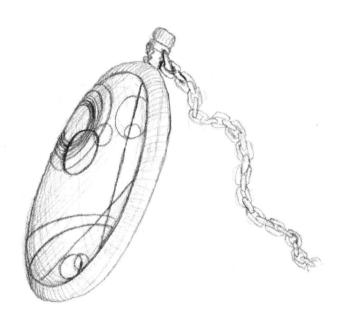

3.9 The Family of Blood

There is no wrath like an angered god
who grants our wishes with storm cloud trod
drenched in kindness, his cold heart swells
dreams written down like the book of Kells
till Morpheus affirmed the end to peace with nods
there is no wrath like an angered God
who lives without that wedding dress or Bells
A field of family he will never sod
drenched in Kindness, his cold heart swells
when friendship dives away your tells
and all you meant was to spare the rod
there is no wrath like an angered god
shivering stageplay humanity along the dolls
a fake Englishman to bring our screams inside our pod
drenched in kindness, his cold heart swells
a family slit by blood to bond in hells
our slumbers Heaven's chains to make us odd
there is no wrath like an angered god
drenched in kindness, his cold heart swells

3.10 Blink

Here
and not
in tears
past the start
we lay down
so our young hands
can wither
to the music of raindrops

3.11 Utopia

I have sunk my hands into clockwork
tuning its mechanisms
grinding fingers to meat
to let those hands point to ten

I wind you up
across the apocalypse
we synch ourselves
like businessmen at the bus stop
I am not a watch
though I am a sentinel
alarm set to burst
when we come together
at the end of all things

four-four time

you can count out our heartbeats
by holding your breath
blowing out air like the stars
our forefathers
turned about like horses
counting off the beat
in four-four time

3.12 The Sound of Drums

I'll break the world beneath my thumbs
You'll hear the noise that I'm its Master
This pounding, pounding, sound of drums

And you think yourself their savior factor
But you just make me tear skies faster
I'll break the world beneath my thumbs

Can't you hear the boiling drums, listen Doctor
hear their song. Are they the choir, I the Pastor?
This pounding, pounding, sound of drums

And this girl you march on warring vector
She'll walk the earth, but I'll in time out last her
I'll break the world beneath my thumbs

While you for thousand years were just reactor
I call on eons, command death, the castor
This pounding, pounding, sound of drums

This world will burn as Troy, with you its Hector
Called from the depths with "Hastur! Hastur!"
I'll break the world beneath my thumbs
This pounding, pounding, sound of drums.

3.13 Last of the Time Lords
Can you hear me calling?
All across the world I walked
I call to you
the story of a Doctor Who
will bring you worlds and dreams
renew your faith in dying dreary
vapid keeling kneeling fools
and raise above the heavens
 you
because the Doctor is the
scourge of those who take away
the rights of liberte
and listens, lies and fights for them

he is the Archangel
to those who think and doubt and spew
their voice with love
and so Love is what we'll do.

I love the Doctor
And though his gaze is never
mine and true
I hope you always love him to.

P Time Crash (#1)
so much celery
makes Belgium holes hard to fill
link with hugs to win

P Time Crash (#2)
oh no you're a fan
get your brainy specs on now
time to patch up time

XMAS Voyage of the Damned
Did you ever hear about Christmas?
I heard it was Satan's day
when men in red suits are burglars
and death knocks on every door

So we sail there today for yule-tidings
on a ship predestined for hell
more maudlin a name wasn't figured
for it sunk back in 1912

the Angels are monsters, the captain's insane
the owner's a cyborg trolly
and so we bid adieu to Kiley Minogue
and drop her down fire and panic

4.1 Partners in Crime
grease
gurgling down burgers
and deep fried Twinkies
pouring out your gut
waving goodbye
a lard pie to the sky
happier than a meal
for childhood obesity

whoever thought
that when you said it was a food baby
you meant it literally

4.2 The Fires of Pompeii

Pounding to the chant of oracles
heads held high in desolation
stone ware mastectomies and amputations
life under a carved facade
of propagandic prophecy
built on the software of truth

burning up worlds
in the calculated attempt
to add words to the dictionary
 with the steely eyed
 wrath of Olympians

Rome wasn't built in a doomsday
 and Pompeii
 like Gallifrey
 is smothered in the crib
 forward in time a monument
 to Vulcan
 and saving four souls

#2

Doctor Doctor
did you know?
that you met your self
and your best friend to
under volcanoes

giving a prophecy
to buy your ship
why did they air this
if it was a high budget
casting reel
fishing in your future

4.3 Planet of the Ood

Ancient Egypt for the Jews
the Confederacy to the Congo
the Spaniards to the natives of America
Rome to the Gauls
and Flesh to Flesh
ignoring any breath
easy enough to call into query
the humanity of those
who come in your way
when your hands strike you lazy
and your compassion has shrunk to negligible
ruining lives for a exhaled breath to suck in

you won't forget
your payback has a name

4.4 The Sontaran Stratagem

I'm very good at born to die
like all my brothers
line by line
we ready as crown fire
and kings are paupers
if you kill them
I'll bite my lips
taste the sweet blood
and riot laughing cut myself
I'm very good at born to die
I cannot wait to do it right

4.5 The Poison Sky
Everythings been brilliant
I was to
to a sense of literal
not usually found
in blue box fiction
I could have remade the earth

But I am poison

locked up in lethargy
crushing the world
keystrokes to conquer
clever boys and girls
in rains like me

I am poison

My loss is to the world
And they will rue missing me
as I will miss
my unanswered prayer
for forgiveness

I am poison

I am my own antidote

With a war-cry to the sickened sky

4.6 The Doctor's Daughter
Family are threads on a burned away shirt
and you remember its warmth
and the cut of the cold
singes you till you shiver
when it never stops snowing
in the Siberia you can't ignore
there is another thread on the floor

4.7 The Unicorn and the Wasp
pages turned and pages rest
and so the quiet graves speak
through a pen and through a hand
unmasking unicorns
with a rusty shoe and glue like glance

that holds Poirot and Marple
leaving maple traces on the dew
that footprints clutter up anew

and mysteries come with pages past
torn to memories
with the gasp
of a drowning wasp
we lose all of the past
in paperback

#2
Most read author in the universe,
ever
well that's something to aspire to!

Hath Way There
bubbling in the muck
near the end of the casualty list
you were Hath way through
but never saw the end
a bit too brave
for a child of the machines

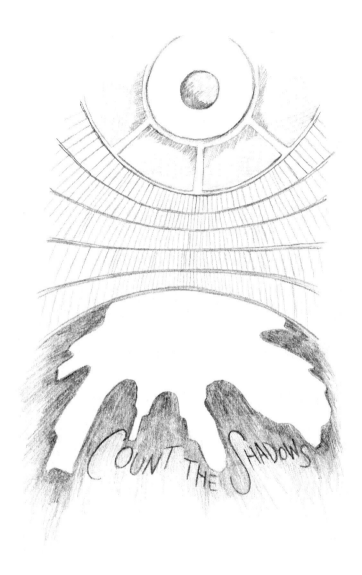

4.8 Silence in the Library
Crunching under bonefoot
in wood pulp cages
gnashing with infinite teeth
and inescapable maws
across caveman sunsets

lift it high to shadows
and the blood sacrifice
of screaming cannibals

4.9 Forest of the Dead
Who is a question
never a namesake
both living by it
medicine man by the creek
and archeologist by the tombstone

wasting away in dreamland
with non-existent children
under the guise of monotony
to hold under wraps
rebirth

a village of no ones and never-weres
lost to a delete key
or a stutter
at the wrong 2 seconds

4.10 Midnight
chime down
and count the clock
no one accounted for
shift on the rock

the shadows cast clockwork sundials
into their winding panic
crank and wound
un unleashed
stroking midnight
with the fury of a foaming mouthed pup

4.11 Turn Left

There have been many turns and violent throws
and many, many ways to go
a different path to breathe his last
and goon no more silent
to loose the curse of open worlds
of dreams so ever pliant
the concrete walkway beckons past
to call you off from Pentecost

there have been many turns and violent throws
and many, many ways to go
so lost so lone
you wander unkempt
and that scratch on your back
is more virile a curse than a dove attack
talons of wasted days dying
so choose at last
there have been many turns and violent throws
and many, many ways to go

#2
many directions
tricky choices for Donna
much in so little

4.12 The Stolen Earth

The Bees are gone
and so is the Earth
so was she at Bad Wolf Bay
and so are we all now today

decade by decade we drip on by
with face that change
but still we live the same old story
repeated by old men at Christmas time
and by gigolos in wood burn bunkers
or women and house urchins

all along the rampart
as the castle is moved by truck
to a circle of alchemy
in the celestial sphere

to transmute bees
into memories

4.13 Journey's End
End to end
all gathered round
Sarah Jane and all her kin
Jack's two buddies, around him
the Doctor's Hand
the Doctor to
Its practically a party
Pinata Mickey, Donna, Rose
and her mom with her new Pete to show
Martha, UNIT, K-9 to
Geez if they can't save the world
We're through!

End to end
all Gathered Round
one switch to flip, six hands down
the ship that was flown
by a lonesome God
is now a home
with a family round its center
its panels and turns
holding Earth firm
till they can all
surround
a camaraderie bound

4.14 The Next Doctor

The face of your Tomorrows
blinks and breathes
gasps at the forgotten mask
of who you couldn't be

stare into that man
who has hailed your failures
into a pitiless smile
that eggs on your swift sorrow

but he isn't you, your flesh cannot be
more than this day, or this cusp
when you push your glasses to your brow
and exclaim into the height

with your own voice, his
that all of this was worth
a single cheer in the
dying year

Animated Special: Dreamland

Buried in the sand
was a tin foil hat
runed and hollow
crumpled underfoot
with the secrets of the universe

4.15 Planet of the Dead

Bus tour to the end of eternally
make a pit stop at death
everybody dies
though a few of them survive
and a joke or two with the TARDIS

hey there's a spy
look that thief right in the eye
she's going to steal a cup
but it'll be alright
you will use it to survive
when the toothy desert chomps you up

so let's all party
sunshine blood and guts
rite of the equinox
all sacrificed
to bring out a new life
when the tour turns into the station

4.16 The Waters of Mars

You thought you went to the gym more than Atlas
and advise Daedalus on wings and glue
so you put on your Jack-Boots like Bowie
sieg heil to the great white Duke

Lord of all, Victor and King
sure to make survival a thing
shoot all the wolves
and chew on the flock
not duty or reason
objectively God

Atlas is crushed with a planet of Roses
Icarus melts like ice cream
so put on your Jack-Boots like Bowie
and prove that there is life on Mars

they flee from your temple
and walk into the sea
they'd rather drown than herald
your kindergarten Odyssey

4.17 The End of Time Part 1

Alpha
This is a note
In the symphony of Creation
the Chords and reminisces of being
played out by atomic charts
and half wit smokers with beakers
this is one note
this is the note that ends the day

Beta
Gallifrey, torch of the gods
Olympia
 throned of Rassilon
sanction sacrilege
to sacrifice sordid
everything
for the sake of dreams of water droplets

Gamma
would you keep a picture and burn the town?
keep the wallet's smiling family and leave your own?
the image is all they see
when reality is but a memory
at the end of time

Omega
a wife
And you weren't anything without
a wife
a lone prisoner
vacated of your inebriated disturbance
and the cackling of your banter
a wife
who is no longer your punching bag
so get lost to history

Pi
Christmas is good
Grandfather to Grandfather
its always pleasant
except for the aliens, and the apocalypses
but other than that its cheery
and there's the Doctor
what a good man in his Blue Box
if only Donna knew….
well, we all her him a lot.

Sigma
This song is ending
and your note is played once
the Master faces all
and you are just one chord
beneath his screaming melody

4.18 The End of Time Part 2

Gallifrey
10 million years of pinnacle rites
turning sunshine into lightbulbs
and morphing the flow of years
into history books

Gallifrey
No fashion sense
but wonderful sigils
mad glorious eternity
unending and undying
regenerating till the lights burn out

Gallifrey
founded by vanishing
ended by vanishing
its sons locked in a war
against its own existence

Gallifrey
could you die
if your own mother
told you to lose your home

Gallifrey
is gone

Earth
and you've survived
till you hear him knock four times

your heart beat beckons
and all that's left is demise

and the ultimate renewal
of new skin
Gallifrey
Son of its sons, last of its lasts
unburdened in the Geronimo
of living

11th Doctor

5.1 The Eleventh Hour
I washed away a thousand years of life
with fire from my skull
cracking my home
into coral shards of coal
until I become
a children's book character

P Meanwhile in the TARDIS.... #1
Space ship made of wood
its not OSHA compliant
don't inspect it hard

5.2 The Beast Below

triumph of the last great agony
when all you give
is all that is taken
by those you love
submitting to the crown of thorns
for the sake of the little ones
who could not hear your scream
whom you could always hear cry

5.3 Victory of the Daleks

Alive
whats that but a bunch of cells and
maybe a memory or two or a lie
Alive
like her, who waited, who was never born
a fragmentary engagement of the falsities
of pepperpots
Alive
I am always alive, I burn with life, and living,
lost to the limbic system of the universe
utilizing my very breath to tell me
A Lie
I remember her. And it doesn't matter
for in the end
I Am Alive
Because the lies become me
and through them
I Live.

5.4 The Time of Angels

Sweetie, sweetie
High heels like a duckface in a shredder
Lipstick like poisoned honey
hair like miss Frizzle
probably is miss Frizzle
guns, lots of guns
no gum, oddly
my wife, girlfriend, nobody
no one?
someone?
River Song
Sing along
you ain't got much to ring for
you know, in prison.

5.5 Flesh and Stone

can you scale my eye with Prayer?
forlorn Octavian not set to rule
and lost to light (blind, ing)
Christian Medusa's glare
dealt not in marble like their hands
but the gift of long and happy death
until the scar did slash

Angel Bob? Can you hear?
can you smell or feel?
you're just a puppeteer
with slops of meat marionettes

and yet again, your wings
can't flight from light
and did you ever think in your
immortal way
that you would be defeated by
a bedroom wall?

P Meanwhile in the TARDIS #2....

So many faces
old comrades unforgotten
leather bikinis

5.6 The Vampires of Venice

I had a wife, or was going to, was, will, what?
and now we're awkward
and the Doctor's done
quite enough to derail damn and demonize
the idea
I'd ever be good enough
for a girl with her hair like a Celtic warrior princess
and eyes like a brush of skin in the rain
who kisses like--
--he kissed her
and I'm just second finish.

5.7 Amy's Choice

I once had an imaginary friend.
who bundled me off to dreamland
and stole me away like the Erlking
to far off lands, where skies
were made of manners, and city dwellers fish
to the ends the Earth had, the start of wars
and I waited till the sky burned
with dawn

And he was never there,
till I long outgrew my dreams
and in his place a boy who thought ponytails
would make him cool, and dreamed of me,
not skies
till the whole world froze to him
and there was no other guy

5.8 The Hungry Earth

waiting
so
long
so deep
within
curling under its crust
Lizards under rocks
silent
a quiet empire
empirical minds
studied
drawn
dissected
disinterred corpses
sunder Earth
creeping into
your churches
homo reptilian superior

5.9 Cold Blood

under a sky
we were born
and the Earth stayed beneath our feet
and it was so for each of us
from tail to tow and foot to skull
we raised our eyes to sunlight
and cried out as one
in our breathing

you and I are the same
past the differences of skin and taste
we breathe this sky
breath by breath
& taste its meady rivers

we walk an Earth together
bound by our blood
whether boiled or frozen
we live.

5.10 Vincent and the Doctor

Flowing whirls and swirls
color pearls formed at moonlight
each dab exonerating light
mooring the sundials of the sky to architects
craft the world in oils
as it was dreamed and as it soared
petty definition be damned
for flowers are more than the vein of a petal
and a face holds a soul under rotting skin
a beaming pulse in canvas
smeared sky brights stars that dim

candles beneath the black cloak
that courses through,
soaring out in blue, red, gold
and twisting in time
to choreograph our astrology
and the geography of the matrimony
of our feet to the soil
with the slight slick strokes
of a magician's brush

5.11 The Lodger

How do you humans do it?
Is this a towel or a Toga?
This toothbrush says its sonic...
I wasn't aware that you were prepared
to brush your teeth like a Harkness!

cooking things? That's a snap, I learned that
from—Oh is that a soccerball?
football ho! Scoring goals
and other human things
like washing up
and dreaming of Monkeys

I never stick around too long in one plane
jumping between worlds like hopscotch
square by square
as you scuttle down the pavement
small as oysters
large as whales
forging empires with bunkbeds

5.12 The Pandorica Opens

I once had an imaginary friend.
His name was Zeus. Only he wasn't
so unreal as to make me
by his children's hands.
And as a gift upon my Vulcan-forged birth
a box
to never see nor open
...but just a peek.

I once had an imaginary friend.
His name was the Doctor. Only I don't
think he really had a medical degree
he found me to hold onto when my
family was nowhere
and I waited
and I waited
but his blue box was left ungifted
till I had given up
and its doors opened into eternity

I once had an imaginary friend.
Her name was Cleopatra
and she kissed me crazy
till a Legion fell to her knees
and then she flowed away into
--like nothing at all--
an endless stream

I once had a girlfriend.
and then I died
or ceased to ever die
    or nothing
and then I was
like a remolded toy
standing on the banks of the Rubicon
between reality and playtime

I once had a mad man in a box
and now he is so again
packaged away
like a Christmas present
forgotten amidst the druid ruins
of a half canceled Ragnarok Apocalypse

There are no stars.
There are no stars.
There are no stars.
There are no stars.
There are no stars.
There are no stars.
There are no stars.
There are no stars.
There are no stars.
There are no stars.
There are no stars.
There are no stars.
There are no stars.
There are no stars.
There are no stars.
There are no stars.
There are no stars.
There are no stars.
There are no stars.
There are no stars.
There are no stars.
There are no stars.
There are no stars.
There are no stars.
There are no stars.
There are no stars.
There are no stars.
There are no stars.
There are no stars.... But in my dreams.

5.13 The Big Bang
There are moments where
the universe is a Carnivore
and what you love is fed though
its slaughterhouse teeth
to the meat soaked ruins of your dreams
and where the last light in the universe
is the same that's drying you to your bones

Rise up!

You are a centurion, Guarding Rome
and the very box of Pandora herself
you are the most important woman to be born
whom whole realities are crassly conjured for
you are that woman as a child, yearning
for destiny
you are a mystery, and a melody,
and a flowing stream to wash away hell
you are a mad man with a box

And you can correct the malfunction of malevolence
and dethrone the sharpest tooth and
tackle the tiger by the tail
Because You are the beginning
all of you
are the start of a world more
sizable than Rome
because you are you
and through your hand
the old and beaten path
will explode.

XMAS A Christmas Carol
Fish swim where you heart is
the frozen nodes of the sky
become Atlantis
forever hanged by the day
the only day
the one that comes without morning
where you lock her up in hospital beds
and call it medicine

riding sharks into the horizon
to greet Jolly Old St. Death
with a carried cruciform of cheer

P 1 Space
a TARDIS in a
TARDIS that is not good no
ouroboros, me

P 2 Time
oh dear a spare Amy
not that she minds her own face
with a wink and nod

P Death is the only Answer
Hey look its Einstein!
No don't turn into an Ood
avoid demise please

P Prequel to the Impossible Astronaut (#1)
No monsters in the
White House slipping away my
memories, no way

P Prequel to the Impossible Astronaut (#2)
Scary monsters here
dressed up to the nines
Nixon can save me

6.1 The Impossible Astronaut
Gods don't die
they fade into storybooks
where little children chant your name
and hold up flashlights as screwdrivers
to turn the heavens one way or
another
No, Gods don't die
Not if you remember them

#2 - My best friend Nixon!
Tricky Dick is a tall ordered man
look at him bigoting his way through Washington
stuttered and frustrated
and off to the moon

but won't even let you get married by noon
Tricky Dick is a tall ordered man
look at him trembling
all paranoid plans

6.2 Day of the Moon
I am the wrath before I was wronged
the innocent knife cutting horrors in prongs
and verse to flow not into sequence do
Time is around us, streaming though

Death comes to everyone
gods and silent masters
one by one they'll turn on you
humans, wives, and last... her?
 No, never her.
She's waited long enough as it is.

P Prequel to the Curse of the Black Spot (#1)
yo ho ho and a
we're all dead with a
high spot of trouble

P Prequel to the Curse of the Black Spot (#2)
waves ever so calm
dead ship in a deader sea
the plague spreads

6.3 The Curse of the Black Spot

The skin of a mirror
below your barnacles
patched to eye the silver
stolen from Pharisees

the skin of a woman
long forgot at sea
calling Odysseus
strapped to the mantelpiece
reminders of home
in the pulse of lust

Odysseus sailed against Poseidon
you fight band aids
and the curse of corruption
marked for a hospital bill
you can only pay with decency

6.4 The Doctor's Wife

I was sexy
before I was a history book
marked down for scrap
like a disowned sorority

sexy TARDISES
all dressed up in pretty dresses
and flesh suits
putting their best breast eyes nose heart
heart lungs feet bones and venison
for the vortex ballroom

dying TARDISES
wearing away for a Surgeon
a doctor who waits on them
and takes them away

thieving TARDISES
looking for a larcenist
must love adventure
(spot filled)

6.5 The Rebel Flesh

Bubbling skin in cauldrons deep
bless the lord and damn him deep
tan the hide to let it dry
and walk in flesh both yours and found

in the pot put sulfur to, hydrogen
make protein stew
stir the science magically
to birth a baby woman free

new MacHeaths now, everyone
to open up corroded dawns

6.6 The Almost People

They have been you
the scorned, the poor, the Jews
the blacks, the brown, the women
the Indian, the sweatshop workers
the child slaves, the prostitutes
the Chinese workers who jump out of
windows to make your iPads
and the Bangladeshi women
burning up to stitch your
sneakers

Screaming as the flesh boils off their bones
the almost people you never see
because you cover your eyes
to seal yourself in the cocoon
of your iPod
your fingers slipping off its bloody surface
running your tired fingers along its rebel flesh

P Prequel to A Good Man Goes to War (#1)

you don't have a head
medically that is bad
get that looked at sir

P Prequel to A Good Man Goes to War (#2)

Judoon brain, boxed
don't sell to monks with no
heads, that is creepy

6.7 A Good Man Goes to War
She was yours to protect
and you lit up your manhood like a bonfire
pounding your chest
and prepping your (clever) banter
to wrestle armies with jokes
and unleash the Golden Horde
to pillage the Anglicans
like a sterilized Viking

You mow them down
with milk maid nurses
and lesbian lizards
building you tower
of unbleached skulls
without a severed spine
King of the Storm

without a hope of victory
against the last breath
of a too-wanted child

#2 Mommy
Oh, there you are.
And there you've been.
How I've waited through your uncaring eyes
to see you knowing me
and all I see is shock
I was your friend, your baby
and now I'm here
yes, I've kissed the Doctor...
yes, its serious....
I've waited my whole life for your embrace
and it has to happen
as I've been taken away

P Prequel to Let's Kill Hitler (#1)
he said he'd find her
will he strike down heaven for
a mother's tear drop?

P Prequel to Let's Kill Hitler (#2)
alone and searching
no baby for their bedtime
pick up the phone, doc

6.8 Let's Kill Hitler

I dreamed I had a daughter
she could hold my finger with her whole hand
and she slept against my breast
and she was real
and she was lost

but what is my daughter now?
and when can I hold her?
is she
but a paradox
a ruined childhood
sacrificed for the silence
of a question never asked?

and now we're killing Hitler
or he's killing her
dead and born again
in the furious upkeep
of motherhood

6.9 Night Terrors
little boy now don't be afraid
the monsters will get you for certain its said
you're made of wrong things
alien slime and cuckoo sings
on the chime
of sticks and snails and puppy dog's tails
and the riot in your mind

so wrong, to live
undeserving of love and outward you
wish for love

--which they give
little son, filled with love
that's what little boys are made of

6.10 The Girl Who Waited

Green Anchor:
where are you?
at the end of the gates I see only plague
at the end of decades where is your hand
and your wrinkled face

Red Waterfall:
dripping down with years
is the crinkle of your skin
and the passé Naivety
of trusting men with medical degrees
for they can tell you anything
perched as herons
from their high bespeckled chairs
they squeak at the bandage bearers
and the water falls down
and I am only anchored
by the nurse they scorn

6.11 The God Complex
What do time lords pray to?
when the storms down your cathedrals
and there is not to face but the rain
where do you step but puddles
when there is no drain

that cool reflective
leaves nothing to the dark
the outlines of your shadow
lie whispering
hollow in their mark

P Up all Night (#1)
terrible father
afraid of that, actually
I need a Doctor

P Up all Night (#2)
will not sleep for me
roughshod baby formula
kids are difficult

6.12 Closing Time
How do you Humans do it?
with baby oil & diaper duty.

I am a force beyond Imagination
darkness eternal and brutality reasonably managed
slayer of the stuffed bunny
and master of my crib
I am the dark lord Stormageddon!
your baby Alfie
(to you peasants)

P Prequel to The Wedding of River Song (#1)
that's many silents
in your Ra Aquarium
where are the fishies?

P Prequel to the Wedding of River Song (#2)
Fed up with fish tanks
such nice suits for aliens
whoa, cool eyepatch bro

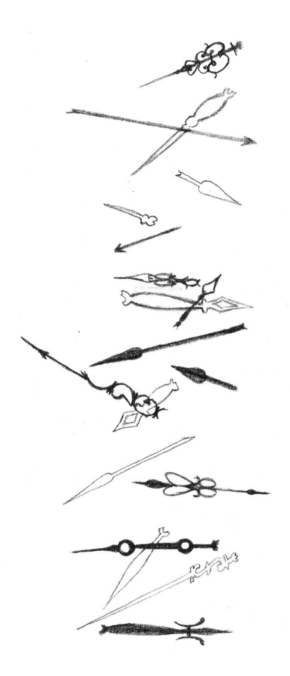

6.13 The Wedding of River Song

You always told me with your eyes
that I was something special
when I'm not
I'm nothing
like an unblinking drool lipped
pantheon of one
for hedgehogs
burrowed in the dirt till you can't make
name nor tail of me
because I deserve to suffer under shutters

so stop telling me I'm worth
it
and tearing the hands of clocks off
to hold me tighter than I deserve
stop it
till you flow into my heart
like the untempered stream you
are

and I don't deserve you
and who cares if I want you
but you love me

and every star in the sky stutters to
tell me that again.

P Prequel to The Doctor the Widow and the Wardrobe (#1)
pick up your cell phone
this space ship is going to...
BOOM.... I am alone

P Prequel to The Doctor the Widow and the Wardrobe (#2)
get your helmet on
and leave a message for Pond
Spaceship goes boom now

XMAS The Doctor The Widow and the Wardrobe
Fairy Land is the place
where you lose your name
for the sake of morality
delve into Narnia!
the wicked witch of the poison
draining out roots

wave your wand
glow in the light of the forest
wizard, Druid, Shaman
no layman is he
who ushers those woods
and saves the last dying branch
of the tenable under breath
to exhale it
celestial saplings
an ending of bark into skylines

P Inforarium
erase me to start
then go back to silent ends
erase me to start

P Night and the Doctor: Good Night
Don't play with not your things
Don't keep your queen in fish bowls
It will all end bad

P Night and the Doctor: Bad Night
A good day, bad night
caught in pain, loss, wasting away
ice cream saves us all

P Night and the Doctor: First Night
Hide her from Herself
split up date night for lovers
fork in the River

P Night and the Doctor: Last Night
tick not a heart beat
you know she wouldn't make it
clock is half past dead

P Pond Life (#1)
live life without Ood
but with no running Doctor
would that be folly?

P Pond Life (#2)
in and out he goes
domestic splendor calls away
dinner is cold now

P Prequel to Asylum of the Daleks (#1)
nifty cloak you have!
I do miss the full café
oh no, not Skarro…

P Prequel to Asylum of the Daleks (#2)
bad dream cafe
hooded and cloaked to mire
meeting post horror

7.1 Asylum of the Daleks
I was a Ballerina
tight and twirling
before I was canned like beef hash
and sworn into pieces
Moloch in a tutu gown

I was a lover
so was she
and our fingers used to touch
before they were cut off
and replaced with toilet cleaners

I was a human
and they called me Oswin of Alaska
now I am a tin shell
and a puddle of tears
with no tear ducts

and we are human

7.2 Dinosaurs on a Spaceship

Rawr! Goes the dinosaur
Brilliant! Goes the Doctor
run up all the hallways
there you'll find a monster

Bang! Said the hunterman
Trowel! said the Father
waiting up for dinosaurs
and throwing all the golf balls

Ahh! Said the evil man
Run! Said the Doctor
cold and black and heartless
when you sin against his darkness

P The Making of the Gunslinger (#1)

five inch bolts in each
heart valve and cut off his love
guns don't kill people

P The Making of the Gunslinger (#2)

forged steel
skin like glue from horse hoof
drain away dead man

7.3 A Town Called Mercy

you can't forgive what you can't forget
you want gunsmoke?
go blast through
till you find your peacepipe
out on the range (how strange)
is it that watching you
I'm just the sheriff
who gives up his badge
a secular temp whose meanings been had

but this is mercy
and you can't forgive what you can't forget

so blow up this eloquence
mop up the dissolute vagrants
and mark this town as the hole
of genocide and killers

but this town is mercy
and you can forgive but you can't forget

so put down your gunsmoke
and let it rise up
cause the clouds can
take it off your hands
and walk into a new town

cause this is mercy
and we can forgive... and we can forget

7.4 The Power of Three

Husband, house, job, car, and a Doctor to
living the domestic dreamscape wii planned
except for the soldiers and undergarments

cubes, boxes, black, square, and a steward who
is living the memory of old friends and fathers that manned
the wars and now strive to find these cubic varmints

Days, years, months, hours, and a man untrue
stopping the end of world, but living a family life behind
wasting away in time, and giving away hugs for armaments

7.5 The Angels Take Manhattan
Raggedy man
like a doll a little girl picked up
and set down gently
with an angel's touch

The last centurion
more glorious than a god
a husband
that when it comes between
heaven and love
Angels will weep every day

We saw him die, and we kill ourselves
to right the end
and rear our adopted children
in the godless past
called New York City

#2 - Bye bye, Pond
You were the first face
that fed me breakfast
and the last face
that wished me well
and now you are a hollow name in a rock
and a million days we never shared
over custard
dipped in fish
or the other way around...
without you
where do I face at all?

P The Battle of Demon's Run, 2 Days Later (#1)

Strax is not dead, which
relieves us of the burden
to miss his wit so

P The Battle of Demon's Run, 2 Day Later (#2)

Sleepy Sontaran
wake up now little guy for
adventure is near

P The Great Detective (#1)

I'll blow up the moon!
No? Not good enough for you?
I need more grenades...

P The Great Detective (#2)

invade the moon for
friendship of the dearest sort
lonely made up tale

P Madame Vastra Investigates (#1)

two lovers in green
sharing adventure and fun
with kisses at home

P Madame Vastra Investigates (#2)

catching the crook
cold blooded detective with
warm beating heart

7.6 The Snowmen
Childhood is such a fragile thing
and all it takes are snowflakes
chilling out you tongue
to hollow your adult hood
into plaster and Victorian circuitry
and the windchill of sideburns
and a too-brimmed hat
shielding your heart
from the warmth of December

Not a cup of cocoa
in the frozen cup
when you awaken
to find your years drunk

P The Rain Gods
Sacrifice for crop
water and medicine man
forecast is soggy

P Prequel to The Bells of St. John
lost a lot of things
mojo, but not a friend
hope you can find her

P Prequel to The Bells of St. John
I lost my mojo
and my gran, pencil, Clara
I got it back though

7.7 The Bells of St. John
you died and died and here you are
and death will pass you by
with a wave and toothy smile
as you kiss the children goodnight

so being dead, your life is short
so breakfast time it is again
eating in a café
and drinking cappuccino
to wake you up from an early demise

so live your life on quadrocycles
fly and run and taste like the leaves that
float in their downfall

we're not particularly great, or intelligent
 but we are alive
ringing in the new year
 with an oversized mobile phone.

7.8 The Rings of Akhaten
Pray, Doctor Dear
for darkness is diligent
 desolate in its scope
 to encompass and caress
 a lotioned thorn
 to twixt you kindly
 to venomous applause
Hope, Doctor Dire, for
Darkness is Diligent
 &the last song
 is no river
 is remorse
 is the same
 is the vanished future
of last month's heresy
and the hymns you herald into the ears of maple trees
to grow out
and fill in the last screams
over a never pushed swingset

P Clara and the TARDIS
over and over
cannot sleep with that blue box
showing me to me

7.9 Cold War

We're all in the Night of the sea
prowling like we were meant to be
hungry like the wolf

building bombs to level land
to keep the peace at hand (and paw)
howl at the moon
Red soil and blue sea collide
a battle song we will provide
hungry like the wolf

were you a parent? I was to
do you think your daughter would smile
with you
out on the prow
hungry like the wolf

7.10 Hide

Romeo and Julie-ahhhh!
what are you keeping from me?
past the glasses and the lost medallions
I see the way you see me
like I was millennia away
from every shell and shot
and bloody mess
and the screams at night that keep you shattered
and I wait

this machine, I think its broken
To see back, to catch a glimpse
to mark the depth the spirits sank
to run my hands through death
and pick out the cracks in its skulls
too long the circuits crumble
and I see the break in the system
reflected in the screen

7.11 Journey to the Centre of the TARDIS
There is a depth at the center of the world
when the machines of the gods
are deus ex machina
to your belief
forging books of bubbles
and laughter from iron
to encase your burning flesh
in a loop back

there is a depth at the center of the world
a pounding engine
like falling till the sky scatters
into butterflies

7.12 The Crimson Horror

Monster, my monster
if bloody eyes could see
what would your horror be?

Mother, my mother
hands like hooks and gnarled breast
violent familial sanctity

Doctor, my Doctor
setting me free
and would I live past this test

Monster, my monster
what would your horror be?

7.13 Nightmare in Silver
Move 1:
In all things, I become
from wasp to titan
I lay back
sinking psyches
pooled around my chest
dipping into memories
and formless regret

Move 2:
resurrected as a bent and broken funhouse
to corner my past
in gold trimming
running up thy CPU
to cool it with Cyberiad

Move 3:
screwdrivers are no substitute
for stethoscopes
or anti-virus software
for your skull

Check:
She doesn't want to be queen
 but it's your move
and I'd love to
 we are the circlet in her crown

Checkmate
Long ago and far away
the Cyberiad came to play
building a toyland
of vivisection
that lost out to Willy Wonka
and Nuclear Bombs

P She Said, He Said (#1)
life could make sense
Till we go to Trenzalore
memories future

P She Said, He Said (#2)
start a mystery
wander through our memory
end at Trenzalore

P Clarence and the Whispermen (#1)
faceless eldritch one
waiting calm in jail cell
Lovecraftian horror

P Clarence and the Whispermen (#2)
hush no more killer
great intellect has you bound
as a tattle-tale

7.14 The Name of the Doctor

2.
I made a promise
to Roses by Ponds
and the friend of god
Nobles and healers
who waited on me with potatoes and lizards
but it was all about Jenny in the end
we walked to my Grave for Jenny
by my politely dead wife
and there she was
awaiting renewal with a cold pulse
all because I wouldn't say my name

1.
I was an impossible girl
born and dead in the same instant
with a long life
on Earth and Gallifrey
I poked out of the stars

we walked to his Grave for my questions
for my mysterious unlogged fortitude
for Time Lord I was
and the deaths I shouldn't be again
all because he wouldn't say his name

-3.
I made him a widow
which is more than
most wives can say they've done
for their hubbies
I get results

He walked over my Grave for Jenny,
the lizard woman's wife
working with his teeth clenched
so I could say his moniker

4.
I made a promise
and spread it throughout time
when I stopped being Grandfather,
    & became a physician
panacea and Aesculapius
to every soul
yet to breathe
hobbling across the sky
in a one-wheeled chariot

and I lost that promise
years ago
staring into Night
like it would switch on
if only I broke down into savagery
and was played by John Hurt

3 THE DAY AND THE TIME

P Night of the Doctor (#1)
So good to see you again
and say goodbye
to all the days you only spoke of
drinking a cup of Hurt
to end the long drought
of those wilderness years

P Night of the Doctor (#2)
Eight is back again
but he will not be alive
long so enjoy it

P The Last Day
Gallifrey burned
and our last hope for safety
foresaw it away

The Day of the Doctor

No More

"No More", he said, and no more there was
like words whispering over the water
for just a moment
he muttered words into fire, and the fire was light
and the light burned like glass
with the pale reflections of strangers
and a billion tiny faces

Monsters are real, they said before
their words echoing over cradles
shushing themselves early into their mornings
and wishing they'd heard it in the evening

crushing the coal in their stockings
on the trudge to school

wondering who the monsters were they'd talked about

but despite it all, they grew up

as we all do with broad faces and thin faces and stubble on
chins and legs

we said, No More, but few had the decency to act on it

if it was decent at all

Decency
decent people are rarities
of the kind you don't usually find
pick them up and run with them

like seashells singing the ocean

you can hear it again
when you thought you had lost the song

Motorbikes
decent people like motorbikes
not to say other things aren't good

like feet or cars

but motorbikes, like bowties

are cool

But despite all of that, the ruination of worlds is beyond the
means

of motorbikes and cool

and when decency becomes desperation
what can a good man do?

"Do not speak of how to be a good man-"

I have seen the last 10,000 years of desperation pass before
me like a splinterbox filled with my fingers and cut up with
every sliver of the memories I had forgotten I forgot. When I
walked across booted plains with boaring knaves and said "I
am the Doctor" and "I am the Warrior" till I forgot who was
who and let the potions dribble down my chin into a beard
too wyrd for Shakespeare though I hadn't met him yet in all
those centennials of celebratory cavalry. We gallivanted
across the eons with our boxes and our consoles with no
one to console the cast of Caliban of me, eternally hurt, at
least for the Day.

And day by day we drew it on across that void and into the
planes. We're coursing through our silent hours and casting
off the memories of me. Wiping me clean like you're pulling
up a new tabula rasa with all your new fangled bow ties and
tied off tennants of terrible torment. You twirl along in your
sand shoes and sandwiches and survey the surreys of time
with hourglass figured firebrands in your eyes. You burn
and burn and burn and say you're not like you were as you
let the fire run across your hands and into the bandages you
left behind as an apology.
But you're not Apollonian, and too far from Aesculapius to
be a Doctor.
You're just doctoring your image to turn away the heat you
lit yourself.
Firing away the last real danger to furnace the wrath of

untold tales. Losing years with every blink to get so so so so so tired in how tied up you are to the passage of the past.

And it was past, till you took me there.

Took me there again when I didn't want to go.

To the showdown of all of us and myself.

Where blind men go to pray to empty gods and nurse their wounds.

A pool of narcissus where we can all stay standing.

And admire the way we failed that day.

But not before we find fezzes! Or maybe that's to late, or is it early?

Hello, again, old me! With your beard, and the other one with too much hair gel.

We'll he's one to talk when he has no taste in interior decoration.

I quiet myself, in triage, and send out the seal in triplicate. I am a replicant of my own image, a Zygon on a horse that is a horse to be a horse when I see a queen. But we're all playing at royalty. Fudging our way through the proper role of information and running amok when we're all among friends. Picking up our nitpicks with hand mirrors.

And oh Clara, clear and good as osmosis, osculating back and forth between six hands. Running through corridors to TARDIS temporal interiors, and how many faces you must see of me... How many times must you gaze at my face and say "see here, this is that man" and manage to close your eyes and believe it when I can't believe me myself. I've gone on so long, and so much longer than I'd like, and its all about me isn't it? When I coal hill schooled those teachers and laughed my way into the stone age through a detour on Skarro and marked Polo all the way to moonbases and Mars

where I wrote my own story of me in Rapunzel's hair and ran away home where they sent me off without dinner and another new face to army bases and lizard men raising Lazarus to find myself off again and on again and writing tin can genesis with faces of evil and winding my way to a Logopolis where I found enlightenment, Kinda, caving myself in to mysterious planets and courtrooms as my own jury and then to remembrance at the circus and cursing Fenric to the day I finally celebrated new years and opened my eyes to harmony, and then forgot myself in blood and rage, till I tired, and was absolutely fantastic on Big Brother and wasn't even the weakest link to doomsday and goodbyes, and so many cries, and if you blinked you'd miss my humanity for what it was and the end of Time and there I was again opening Pandora's box and winding through Rivers.... All from Gallifrey, to end at Trenzalore..... A to Zed, Alpha Centauri to Omega the engineer.... Time Lord Victorious.

The Doctor. Me.

The Winner who lost everything.

Cursed to fight a war I could never win, on a day I could
never lose sight of, with a cost I could never forebear.... Till I
got a second chance with the howling of a wolf.

Howl Away, Rose Red Reveler
Button up your violence into a thing I can bop

and burn away the universe again into the easy answers I
always craved.
Just one push.
And one bark.
And it bites.

"Be one"
But that was always the easy mark
killing, and being that man with the gun
when there should have been another way
when monsters bite you don't bite back
but show a better way to live your life
and push back the tides of ill reason and dissonance
say "this is right, and this is just, and I will do what
must be must, but I will trust in good and love
and not give up
and not give up."

The Doctor
He has been called so many things
A warrior, a healer, a mad man with a box
but whatever he is, whatever he does
he finds something wrong
and makes it okay
maybe it is not good,
or fixed, or right
and rarely perfect,
sometimes he has to fight,
but he always makes it okay.

And never leaves till what was wrong
is gone once more
and the people there
have been given the chance
to endure

Pain
sometimes there is loss
and friends pass away
shoved out of doors

or their thoughts wiped away
but all of that loss just makes him the man
you can trust to say "No More"
with injustice at hand.

Zygon
Oh dear, its you and its me
and we're all evil
pending which side of the table we're on
but a flick and a wave
and we all have the same right to live
despite our sanctimonious death
planned in zeal

a perfect peace, for once, for real

Elizabeth
Throwing confetti!
Isn't it grand?
But I don't think the Doctor
is a marrying man

Paintings
Just like Vincent always said
there is more to the canvas than
light would first show
and into that swirl of colors we go
into the storm of Gallifrey's fall
and away to no more, and nothing at all

The War Doctor
You were so old
So, so worn
killing and fighting
as you'd once forsworn
but that day is done
your day has now begun
and you still have a choice
to be the name in your head
or exactly what you dread

Bad Wolf
she howled away at the nature of creation
barking at the fibers that make up the
time space continuum
and those molecules atoms and vibrating strings
all bowed down to her rule in their sea
sailing the way she told them to
her paws on the deck
slipping into their water
yet never wet
waiting a moment
till she found him so lost
and finding that moment
brought him back to the start

No Sir, All Thirteen!
For oh so long we fought that war
and died and fell
on repeat
rewound and reburied
the Time-War went on
till our Prodigal son came back home.
Everyone of him, for hundreds of years
working to save the home
that jilted he fled
to wander

pacing on the sunlight
like he could be free of light
if only be blinked

and now he comes back, all of him,
one by one
the past, the present, the future,
its all
more wonderful than we could dream of
for when the Doctor calls
sometimes
everybody lives.

Dreams

Clara often asks me if I dream
and I do
I dream of the past,
and a future I'll share with you
tumbling through stars to find home
off on a new journey through unknown toils
finding so many gloried spoils
but taking none
and wandering on
just as the Doctor always has done

The Time of the Doctor
Forward (But No More)
My life began long ago on red fields under an orange sky
running with my toes in the grass,
the trees shining like fire in the morning
and I pushed my hand out
and ran my fingers through time
swimming in its river
Child of Gallifrey
set to run away to new suns and new days
and here I die on Trenzalore

To Adventures
Fleeing across my life
I am a spark igniting my own heart
fragment linked to the shards of truth
that matter to me somewhat more
than I dreamed they would

losing track of the four beats in my chest
and dipping my hands back into that river
seeing a different face every time
casting myself off like an old coat

again and again
till my face has no new clothes to wear

To Clara
You were my saving grace

so many times, and so many lives
you sacrificed for me
and now I see why
in these children's eyes and love
that life isn't all jumping around and dodging danger
sometimes life is walking into death
for the sake of something worth never smiling again for

And you'll get your Christmas goose and Christmas dinner
and pop your crackers with funny hats
and I'll get a whole planet of Christmas
so don't worry about me

To Barnable
No, no I wont leave you
I've left so many times
and so many places
I've had no home
No home till Christmas
and my days of adventure are at an end
I will see no more stars
and no strange new skies
but live and die under these stars
for you Barnable, and for everyone
I am staying for Christmas
for the sake of life itself

To Tasha
Psycho space nun
exactly my type
if I had a type
but you're untypical yourself
sending your confessional priests along
forgetful paths
and sorting me out again and again

but what a good thing
to set your crusade
to save a world
rather than destroy it!

Even if they tried to kill me--
I don't mind.
Silence is only the enemy
if we're not on your bed
eating the pink marshmallows
together

To the Daleks
I never liked you.
You talk really slow.
Get better spaceships, what is this,
Martians attack? Flying Saucers?
Come on Daleks!

PS: You sound funny and
your noses are your eyes
does that bother you?

To the Time Lords
Found you! No longer hide and seek champions!
Floating along in cracks
and calling my name
I never wanted to go home
not till home was long gone
and now you're locked away
but you are safe
at Christmas

To Amelia

oh, there you are, Amy
how long has it been, and
how are you here?
Never mind that...
its been so long,
and all my faces
all my hearts
have beaten away
get your suitcase packed
and come away with me
on one last adventure
before this face
is another's

To Me

Don't forget
You can run forever, for a thousand years
but never forget
you had a place to stay
on Trenzalore
and your hearts will beat again
in four-four time

Love... The Doctor

PS: I won't be gone long!

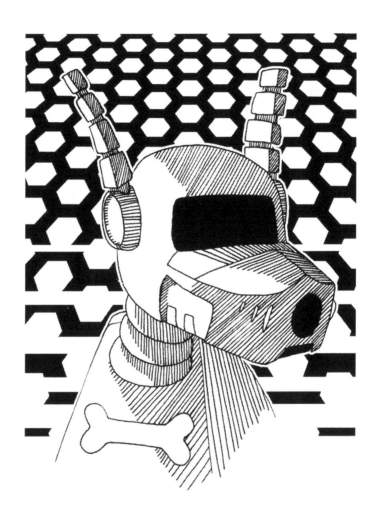

310

4 SPIN OFFS

Spinoffs!

K-9 and Company
1.1 A Girl's Best Friend
holy in that Pagan fall
we sap the harvest, and give to Baal
yet that's the foreign way to say
Cerrumos calls for Athame
and Chalice, brimming with our pride
for blood along the countryside

so shoot the Pagans with lasers
(that's one way to end this phase)

but Sarah Jane... Will she return?
With dog enleashed?
Only if the Doctor learns
a friend is the best thing to keep around

Sarah Jane Adventures

1.1 Invasion of the Bane

Its organic!
Just like arsenic
and so are you,
so pulled from your machines
you come out wholesome
You're organic
but only in the technical form
can you breathe the breaths
that your friends aspire to?

--or there could you find a mother
like an exhalation along the water
to show you life you never thought
your clay could be--

You can take in a breath
but never let it out
for so long that the
continents breathe in your rockstep
shaped of lungs and spinning
with the turn of the plants
but never let it go into light
lest you remember
why went down to
Bannerman road to begin with

1.2 Revenge of the Slitheen

Back to earth
smoking gun fart jokes
tumbling them on
sundering daylight
with vinegar dips

1.3 Eye of the Gorgon

Her, to a Perseus
Him, to a snake
writhing around the gardens
with mirrors in our pockets
searching for a homeland
in the empty vision
of so many habits
frozen to a father
Him, to Medusa
Her, to a father
clutching his stone hands
like the child you are

1.4 Warriors of Kudlak

Its all fun and games
till someone is sold into intergalactic pit fighting
but maybe at the edge of the knife
is something far trembling
and laced with regret

1.5 Whatever Happened to Sarah Jane?

She could have been you
but one single day
shoved her into Azrael's hand

it all seems such a cruel trick
death
But that's all it is in the end
when we live on
and she drops off the face of the world

1.6 The Lost boy

shuffled from home to home
playing cards with faces
of mothers and friends
flushing out the appendages
of card cutting
with the home you always should have had
not by blood
but with papercuts

2.1 The Last Sontaran

out of a million
you were one
survivor of the anthill
and dodger of the magnifying glass
still you wander
and sink your pincers
when you should have been running

2.2 The Day of the Clown

dripping with face paint
the pied piper juts along the crib lines
and marks his space with balloons
and blow horns
waiting for blood
on the swingset

2.3 Secrets of the Stars

Could you count in the secrets
of our bodies
with the constellation Andromeda
or Cancer to whittle away
at the Librality of our fate
charging like Taurus
into what was behind our closed eyes
into Greece, and a previous life

James Wylder

2.4 The Mark of the Berserker
There's only so much make in a moment
when you've relived
the pushing of the swing
the empty seat still wasn't filled
letting dinner get cold
in the arms of another woman
the meat and potatoes
cooked up with adultery

still you always come back
wondering why
the spuds weren't
peeled and served
for your deadbeat pleasure

2.5 The Temptation of Sarah Jane Smith
Never a baby long enough to lick a stamp
howling away from mother's arms
Into the gap in the world
where children play with Loki

they were never there enough then
(and won't be now)
kickstarting the engine
to drive away into a 50's haze

leaving only the proudest of orphans

2.6 Enemy of the Bane
Born and never bred
to know not womb nor teat
yet now you serve the mother of beasts
who lurks under soil and cleat
claws sinking into dirt
with a foot holding gaia
uttering magic words
in a scientific display
of holemaking

3.1 Prisoner of the Judoon
Do not park wrong for Rhinos
for Rhinos are rarer than unicorns
but scratch the paint worse than keys

3.2 The Mad Woman in the Attic
Could you come closer?

Could you have been her so many years ago,
back as a pretty girl,
not waiting in the dregs of cobwebs
alone even to spiders
not even a bug to crawl under my foot
could you wait with the witch
for the time to come back again
and fix the calenders
to mark off every day I lived
as nothing more than the failed memory
I never dreamed to its fullest.

3.3 The Wedding of Sarah Jane Smith

with a wheeze and a groan
you turn back in your wedding dress
and find him there again
like in all the times with armored knights
and spiders crawling round the world
you found him in a school yard
ready to run away again
with his fate in his scarf
and his scarf in his footsteps
tripped up and wandering
never saying goodbye till you meet again
with a tin dog taser
glowing at the altar

he wanders in again
and there are no weddings for medicine men
and there are no grooms that come in boxes
only drifters
and hobos with great hair
running about again and again
till you lose your ring
fishing it out of the drain
without a trick to carry on

3.4 The Eternity Trap

fingers like ice and lightening
only a mirror away
hushed on the glass
and squirming through the annals
of flashlights under the chin
you whip off the dust covers of your bed
to sleep over
and wake away the ghosts

3.5 Mona Lisa's Revenge

Leonardo is such a tool
putting me in bathrooms
give me a laser gun-
a hazier one
then the last exhibit before
cracking out of custody
into the great beyond
I'm a free paint
egging you on the smile

3.6 The Gift
So much to be given
forfeit in a swirl of lies
and half thought out truths
I plant your garden-
azaleas and weeds
but its all weeds
and so were you
which is what I get
for that rash of negligent trust

4.1 The Nightmare Man
dab the Caligari on
when its doubtful that was a child at all
forming newspaper gospels
of your surefire lonesomeness
printed on your powdersilk cheeks
to ravage us with the hope
we might amount to less
than our Nightmares

4.2 The Vault of Secrets

In the 1960's I saw a man who was not a man who was a
man and in that man I saw something beyond what I saw
that was to say nothing except for whispers and cannons in
the palm of your curiosities and that was a man or was it a
man only in the barest sense did I know that in falling apart
we save the next generation by staring into the sky and
soaring our souls out into silent and serious solemnity; but
who could say for certain if those tight black suits were
anything but shadows or the searing sordidity of my shallow
ambition to know what was beyond that door, and every
door.

4.3 Death of the Doctor

leaving so many faces behind
tear wet faces
snarling faces
dead faces
smiling faces
glowing faces
eyes widened faces
towering faces
cowering faces
this face and that faces
running facing this way and that way
supplanting himself so many times
with so many people
and so many lives
turning out his pockets one by one
to line them with graveyards

4.4 The Empty Planet

Clani was here, and Clani was there
and no one was rightly everywhere
dusting the empty alleys
for any surveillance of survivors

but we're so mechanical
crowning our princes
in the empty halls we call orchards
waiting to pick out the fruit
of a thousand days cloister
and two names enjoined

4.5 Lost in Time

A Queen is a Rani, but timeless in books
written down on pages and forced into memory
she sits in her year, but she can only count down the days
though she does not know the time
turning the pages one by one
minute by minute in a nine-day line

A lady, a Jane, no more Grey than the blush
on her short lived cheeks
ready to say goodbye
and only sweet sixteen in 1553

only a girl, and only a Queen

4.6 Goodbye, Sarah Jane Smith

Who could ever replace you?
Not for the sake of mothers or wives
could anyone drive
Bannerman road
without the sound of lipstick
and a quaint little car

5.1 Sky

sing me siphon off
the cold war
let me hold your hand
with mutually assured destruction
can I tag you it
for genocide?

Built up from the playground
little girl Lucifer
bringing light to the Sky

5.2 The Curse of Clyde Langer

build up bridges
put 'em on the streets
totem to the masses
speak it deep

eaten by the dragon
it comes at night
run run run
before it bites

shivering cold
alone and hated
always the fate
of Clyde Langer, vetted

by Clani and the skeleton
she never saw
left on the corner
like she was before

5.3 The Man Who Never Was

leaving aside the Sky,
who was always watching over us
we were cast off waiting for the replicants
of our own families
only to find that nothing was so certain
as the trust of our hugs

there were always liars, and there will be more
there were always horrors, and they will multiply
but even when we lose you, and lose our sight
there will always be the trust
of a woman who can stand up to starlight
and stare up to the Sky, and welcome her down
to hold her tight
and form children not into guns
but people
winning the war she never thought
with not but her own strength

Torchwood

1.1 Everything Changes
its such a cool trench coat
it wipes your memories
which is a perk when
pet pterodactyls plummet
perilously, the dead come and go
awarding the hand
to drag them out of darkness
into more of the same

1.2 Day One
You thought a Kiss would
matter more
in the endless mating season
it wasn't worth the slobber

1.3 Ghost Machine
could you find that justice
that lays on the beds of ghosts
whispering their injustice
into an empty night
heard only by the mute gravediggers
and the wide eyed sociopaths?

Could you hear their cries?
Or would you tear them down
Into the concrete of the soil
with knives
and a continuation
of the cycle of man to ghost.

1.4 Cyberwoman
bondaged and bandaged
fluttering in the coal mine
ensnared and caged
by a love too needy
and unwilling to let go

the leftovers of a woman
a dinosaur,
but no match for one

1.5 Small Worlds
would you go to fair elf land
oh daughter, oh me dear
to be buried in their laughing sand
that my line would never hew

to grow old, you ne'er will
with on your back, new wings
your kin waiting on the sill
to cough up roses as she sings

"to fairy land, to fairy land
where all the candy is at hand
and eyes are gouged out with our thumbs,
that is the way the fairies come!"

1.6 Countrycide
We killed Genghis Khan
and wiped the world with flood
but still its fun
to call up tear drops
like a rain dance

that is, if you're nuts

1.7 Greek Bearing Gifts

shifting her seduction
gender bent parts
Troilus and Cressidas
across her body
kissing with lips that fib
and finishing the day
like a succubi

1.8 They Keep Killing Suzie

over and under the fabric of life
you rise & rise & rise and die
a knight gauntleted
against the ever impending
and never ending doom

stopping your heartbeat
as casual recreation

1.9 Random Shoes

Its a pity you weren't
anyone like who they treated you
plucking out unrelated
photoshops
when you should have seeped away ages ago
fading into the light
by the soul of your sneakers

1.10 Out of Time
she was like the sunshine
on the silver chrome
of forgotten wingspans
fraying teabags
and letting the decade
slide away
into a Sunday train ride

1.11 Combat
Fists up!
And a nip and upper cut
pant and let the sweat on your brow
filter through the air
like snowflakes

land a blow
and bare your teeth
never so far from an animal
 as the insects we are

1.12 Captain Jack Harkness
taking the stone
he infused it with cuttings
and labored to simulate
the first stone
its grooves and snakes
its colors and swirls

but failing that
he threw the first stone
into the river
and all we remembered
was the carving

1.13 End of Days
Death was disappointing
less than the Angels
harmony joined hands
and spirit song birds
surging through
light headed haze

there was nothing

not even the spur to dig in your back
just the long silence
of the loss of life
and the deep rumbles of Abbadon

2.1 Kiss Kiss, Bang Bang
You never got so good a kiss
as the ones that leave the bottles broken
and the chairs tipped
in wild abandon
who needs a room
when you've got lips

2.2 Sleeper
Identity cards
and numbers
prove your facebook pages
and the name on your doorstep
not really who you aren't though
never one step away
from turning off the blinders
and admitting you've been waiting too long
to tell your loved ones

you were always gone

2.3 To the Last Man
scream so gently
and cover it up
pillow rest your head
and press it down
whittling holes into machine guns
to blow you away

2.4 Meat
Chopped and diced and sliced and bits and bits and bits
steaks and wings and thighs
caged and screaming
overgrown with steroids
plopped on the table
without a shame of regret
your cheeks are rosy
with butcher's blood

2.5 Adam
So the best!
Where your friends were comrades
and your comrades were co-workers
who is he but the best of them all
the triumph of ingenuity from genetics
and the national educational system?

How can you not have faith,
when such a man kisses the earth with his toes
deluding it with plastic jewlery

2.6 Reset
you cannot kill a hive
if you're the queen
unless you have divine decree
(which sort of comes with monarchy)

2.7 Dead Man Walking
Martha!
Oh, how good you are to see
dressing up the world in medical Jargon
like a Stewart of Home living
even while we're touching up corpses
 it just feels warmer
 to the cold dead touch

2.8 A Day in the Death
there is only so much you can do on a slab
your skin gangrenous
your mouth filled with stagnant air
the flies taking a fancy to your stink
walking with the crunch of fingers
there is no single sunrise
warm enough to turn your skin
into anything resembling compassion

2.9 Something Borrowed

oh so white
she wears a veil
to cover up the other man between her legs
and medicates him from memory
with the smile of her bars
never leaves her job
even on her wedding day
oh so white
she wears her veil
and though she's covered up the pain
she chooses him after all
 over strange

2.10 From Out of the Rain

children of celluloid
withered hands pucker that reel
and turn it past the silent age
into naked digital with quivering privates
chortling like Hamelin
grand larceny of innocence
tucked away in film cans

2.11 Adrift
oh where are you now
my gray hair lost son
could you find no trail
to walk your feet home?

Over field house and
forest your mother
awaits with kisses
and warm foot on plates

Oh child, come back to
your mother back home
but your eyes are so
empty, cold, alone

scream, then.

I wish I'd never found you

2.12 Fragments

our lives
  only moments
forget one
  and
you lose
  the picture
puzzles without pieces
(no one brought the box)

scattered in the wild
like fragments
of your pigsty dream
guzzled in hog throats
like a ticking time bomb

2.13 Exit Wounds

you can only play so long
yet
here you are with all your friends
and soon so less than that
the recess from danger peters away
without a wendy
putting the ball away
with lethal force
as you struggle to kick up from your grave
you lost so many of yourself today

3.1 Children of Earth- Day 1
couldn't you kill them
if the gold shined enough
to put on your vestments
sacrificing the infants in secret
for the supplication
of drug addict gods

#2 Kill your (Wendy) Darlings
When old age wastes Wonderland
till the war crosses running water
sucking out the vampirism
to never never land goodbyes
hush your darlings in the night
and rest their weary heads
on smothering pillows
before they get too old and bold--
--always kill your darlings

3.2 Children of Earth- Day 2
Ode to Frobisher
You pushed that pencil farther and farther
till it rolled off the table
your hands shaking
as your government sanctioned salary
softens none of the seriousness
and those pennies you threw in the coffers
give you nothing but a hard pat
to shove you into the furnace

#2

Pinching his spectacles
focused with the weight of an island
to measure gold
to sell off Hector
to push that pencil one inch further
sweating out a load of
bureaucratic sorcery
unaware of the plagues outside Troy

3.3 Children of Earth- Day 3

decimate, like the Romans do
and make your kin
into packs of cigarettes
sold to far off merchants
with a shrug and a nod
as the legion scours the earth
with the cries of babes in their cribs
snuffed out by the sword
of government intervention

#2

waiting past your bedtime
for 4 -- 5 -- 6
    Buckle your sticks
and bounce along into the night
    to the music of pipers
    whose rising smoke
    is only an oven away

3.4 Children of Earth- Day 4

the smell of you is still on the pillows
and I fear the day it fades away
I wake to feel your breath on my face
and find only vents and flutters

if life is too long
you only go to show
that its only too long
when you're not there
to reach for my clock
and grab my hand

3.5 Children of Earth- Day 5

Burn your own blood
throw the years of bottles and
baby diaper
Into the fire

cry your tears
and tell me its worth it
when he's still dead
In the coming years

4.1 The New World
Not into this fray, again!
Hidden away and trying to hide
from helicopters and hell
there he comes again
like no one could scuff his boots
ignoring the screams that
chase him like stray dogs
drawn to that bloody aroma
of his aftershave

4.2 Rendition
how about a coke
to Americanize that poison
that flows though your veins
sputtering out drips of ambrosia spittle
as seven billion gods look at one mortal
with the deepest of ambitions
to once again be like him
seizuring on the padded floor
escaping again to death
only caught up in the hands of Apollo
11 style miracles
as dawn fades away into the

4.3 Dead of Night

where you could only find us in bedsheets
gripping them with ease
as we pulled away our skin
just to reveal ourselves for a moment
languishing in one-sided phone-calls
as the thrust of the matter is lost in sighs
holding you tightly
never to let go
because I always hated California

4.4 Escape to LA

Dead is dead
unless they still crawl
by the skin of their firewalls
coded away somewhere in secrets

we're all just propaganda for someone
a profit margin or error
saving ourselves with blasphemy
to praise child-molesters
and kiss their feet
because it suits our panic

listen to what they say. And buy into their bargains
two for one silliness, and trepidation
unable to leave the circle
eating ouroboros again

4.5 The Categories of Life

Not you, him
shuffled off into paperwork
scuttled babies past their prime
saving a dollar with guillotines
rolling away tombstones
to clear away resurrection
for efficiency

4.6 The Middle Men

When you see
never sit down
when you hear
never turn your back
when you are told
talk back

when the world looks you in the eye
and says, "its good"
as it sloshes through blood and water
Tell it no
Tell it no again.
And if it won't stop
throw the world to the ground
for the sake of raindrops
washing away tears
rather than bloodstains.

4.7 Immortal Sins

falling from air
he came in a cobalt crate
to whisk me off to Neverland
and now you come to
unless the trust is so great
that to be alone is to be a lost boy

but are my wings like Lucifer
when I lift you up, do you live less?

Put me away in my toybox
like I never lived
in starry heavens
dreaming of nowhere
in the embrace
of your anachronism

4.8 End of the Road
Hate Letter to Oswald Danes

We could never love
what never loved
fretting about your hairdo
shining for the cameras
in your dark duties

throwing the children to Moloch again
just like in the old days
you'll be in that furnace to
never regretting why you got there

4.9 The Gathering
on one end,
you could say
things were getting pretty bad
but only a liar would remark
you should never trust the government
as the fires burn away the truth
with no father left to find
what is there to say?
On the other end

4.10 The Blood Line
here we all are, finally
lined up for riddles like Oedipus, Rex
and waiting for that king was Esther
as lost at Gettysburg as Lee, imagining Harvey
Oswald to wait for them all
and a Gwen
overe so patiently waiting for a cuckolding knight
she casts away.
Leaving only a Jack in the box
to be sprung at the last moment
the queen of hearts

and its there in the center
--hold your hand on your chest--
yes, right there?
Feel it beating?
Rip it out!
Tear it forth!
And throw it into the cataclysm of the world.
Dooming us all to the reaping, and ending Azrael's vacation
ending the time of gods a billion
to make two 1942s
business as usual

K-9

1.1 Regeneration
you were reborn from obscurity
into a universe all your own
who can out-stage a lord of eternity
on his own turf

when there is the eternity he forgets
layered in untoppled towers
begging to drop their parliaments
at the bark of a dog

1.2 Liberation
cornucopias of constellations
Cassiopeia to Castillion
word by world in cages
a zoo for microscopes
let out of their petri dish
for the sake of Liberte

1.3 The Korven
to lose your mind
is such an awful thing
drink out of wires and daughters
    the last dreams of touch
    and the longing
        lost in frigid forges

1.4 The Bounty Hunter
your face is two face
with wheels and wheels
of misfortune
forged for photographs
 and smiles based on screams

1.5 Sirens of Ceres
cries in the streets
undrenched Marx
Dublin Saturday Matinees
as stone throw away
from mindful anarchy

1.6 Fear Itself
what once was foreign to wires
is now in its paws
twining around the dog eared pages of history
it always crops up again
amidst the junk
wires of fear
dragging to hell
those who oppose its tremor
as it dodges in cowardice
at the bark of hope

1.7 The Fall of the House of Gryffen

could you expect that specter
to inspect its clothes in tattered array
like your logic come before
its only a smattering of smoke
dissolved in the realization
we are on cold hard rock

1.8 Jaws of Orthrus

staring at yourself
past the mirrors and the shops
you become that foe you fear
doubling your duty
as friend and foe
to right the wrongs and wrong the rights
as any good dog can do

1.9 Dream-Eaters

shhhhh
dream away your sorrows
and pour them into me
for I am your cup and your blessing
and I do not mind if your bottle flows endless
bring to me your sorrowful sleep
and never awaken again
to the sound of our shhhhh
in your poison lullabies

1.10 The Curse of Anubis
dog and god
are only reversed
words away from each other
how better to see oneself
than by a past light
showing the prayers and sacrifice
to a canine messiah

1.11 Ouroboros
wrapped around the world tree
and chewing its own tail
we all fall together for dinner time
bouncing along our fault lines
for a self-sufficient snack

1.12 Alien Avatar
sinking the river
mother earth withers
clutching her veins with poison
as her green hair wilts
and her skin shivers
we only wish to unlock a future
where such a thing is mythology

1.13 Aeolian
as the world slumbers in sufficient peace
paid for with those unused
freedoms you had sitting around
(its not like you were using them!)
the sound of panic hails

from the outside looking in
it seems the world could fall apart again

1.14 The Last Oak Tree
there was so little left, to leave just that
one tree whose leaves could fall like treasures
would we drop off the face of the soil
to find that world
where the right of our loam
was a rite of exhibition
for admission only?

1.15 Black Hunger
chucked away forever and dropped with a sip
and a burp or a lump or a duck
its all rubbish now, eating your muck
filling up the world till it bursts from the cowl
and devours you up with a grin and a scowl

1.16 The Cambridge Spy

now here we are again-- like we started out!
In the year of our start, in the year of our birth
but outside that mode, and incognito
we rush to save the few of us who sort it out

watching the anniversary of our existence
with a howl at the groovy moon

1.17 Lost Library Of UKKO

contained away in endless pages
we watch from the starlight
giving away our library cards
to check out the universe
and checker the past
with escapades and escapes
somewhere on the page of our body

1.18 Mutant Copper

I was built for so much else
but not which I have seen to do
I have seen the idea of myself
and I have called it good
despite the error of ambition
I aspire to exist
amidst the diodes of my brain
I have become Diogenes

1.19 The Custodians

running amok like little green men
and finding the space for spacemen
and arcade anarchy
no one wants to be a segment of a sci-fi serial
when Buck Rodgers is in town
with ray gun ablaze
dressed as a dog
and ready to aim

1.20 Taphony and the Time Loop

so much for sympathy among the chosen
when your bars are rent
you dig in your claws
gnawing into the furniture
as your rise into the sky
holding on by the teeth
steely eyed against the rapture

you could have staid your hands
if only your teeth weren't so tight

1.21 Robot Gladiators
while its one thing to write of tales
or the stories that touch our hearts
unfurl our hearts,
unburden our tears,
this is a tale of a dog who fought
against robot gladiators
not for naught
but because lets be clear
that's really awesome, come on!
Dear oh dear

1.22 Mind Swap
look away from the past
and face the now
or dwell there sickening till you lose yourself
in the depth of the past
and you can't doggy paddle out
but sink, sink, oh so fast.....

1.23 Angel of the North
fall from heaven, like in the time of prophets
and burn that sky to dust motes

wandering around your enemies
with the firmament above
enclosed in ice
they linger on
in menace

1.24 The Last Precinct

when you were the law
and the law is its own mockery
whose job is it
to clear that froth
from the bowl
so all can see?

The burden is clear
is it you, or me?

1.25 Hound of the Korven

what would your cost be
and how would you run from it
ridding yourself of allies to atrophy
for those moments you glimpsed
before you were here
do the old friend's faces
mark you forever
as you tick tock away
bleeding out your time
into a hypothetical fireball

1.26 The Eclipse of the Korven

Here it all is. A dog and his boy and his boy and his girl
and a nutty old man who thought time could be his to
twirl on his fingers
with Korven and K-9
and regeneration
losing yourself in the mock up of history
to find yourself again
when the deeds get the direst
and the foes the worst
whatever your past was
here you are, from the house of Gryffen
a hero once more

And other journeys...

Scream of the Shalka

Drowning out the chatter
we cry for help
scalping the world
as a mayfly surgeon
pricks our forehead
and relegates us to remembering
    a life before screaming

Faction Paradox

I am an unending mask
nesting dolls for faces
forgetting the notion of order
and the order of notion
rubbing in our cold shoulders
and kissing along its back like a missive
we throw over tables
to jumble our faces
tumbling masks
into a carnival of anachronistic anarchy

Downtime

Back again for another (chant)
every second has been lost forever
as it ticks away and back again
stare into timeless sanguine
       your posture is vapor
   and intellect is ether

    there are only bullets
      and arcane orbs
      news stories
      and an incessant loss
        for
        words

1.1 Cyberon
drugs make the floaty man
silver and clear
bubbling up in subconsciousness
for substandard budgets
billions wait out the injections
waiting to replace their limbs
but no one is a doctor here
there is only psychotherapy

1.2 Zygon: When Being You Just Isn't Enough
Sex, Drugs, and Mind-Control
lock yourself into thoughts so low
that demons run your rubber eyes
and morph away your vapid grudge

ruin worlds, and ruin minds
No one ever said be kind

leaving the choice up to you
if that mind you have was ever enough.

This Town Will Never Let Us Go
Send me a Valentine
  wrapped in tin foil
and nuclear launch codes
  rasping to death
    like a baby rattle

1.1 Doctor Who and the Daleks

Running alone though trees like canyons
you were only little once
now it radiates from you
with one heart beating strong
but enough soul for two

1.2 Daleks' Invasion of Earth – 2150 AD

Rage at the hole in the skin of the soil that bore you
and fill it with the clinking clanking machines
that pushed us past robberies
to revolution
waving a red banner
that could only be carried
by old men and their granddaughters

5 COMPANIONS AND DOCTORS AND VILLAINS, OH MY!

Doctors

One
Castaway intentional
with these loathsome savages
locked in a land of refuse
like a fairytale for clockwork

ready to fly, if only he weren't so grumpy
about the prospect of rewrites

Two
No home on the railroad cars
hitching his own rides
wounding his own tunes
stirring his own pot
beneath a hand full of glitter
    thrown high in the sky

Before it all falls down
bunched up together
in our broken frockcoats
    and a last phonecall home

Three
The words "smoking jacket"
The image "suave man of mystery"
The clothes "glam rock"
The training "martial and fierce"
The friends "gun makers and dames"
Profession "Scientist"
Storming down the closed in bars
and sealing away the savages
with an affection as unbounded
as his Ruffles

Four
wrapped up tight
and older than time
just prepared for winter
with a little overkill
there is no charm sweeter than candy
and no whisper as remembered
  as a hat whisking out the door
    and a scarf catching in the lock

Five
Forward to the foreseen
there should have been another way
trudging through the muck
with hapless optimism
put out like incense
with a a snap of celery

Six

Tennyson could not compare
to the color of kings
and a robe to blush Joseph
wandering the desert
with a high chin
and the face of reason
dictated by a charlatan
but never carried to its conclusion

Seven

scheming like a smoke filled room
and the lull of burning at your feet
he catches glimpse of forever
and emasculates it
writhing on the floor
as his sullen eyes show the pity
of no ordinary clown
(as master of ceremonies)

Eight

Dusting off that old book
to turn the page

from Cali to Karn
At a loss for companions
dripping them off like the dust he shook
and loosing those pages into the wind
never born to run--
--but the shoe fit

War
it Hurts so much
as hair shingled away to gray
till the grievances couldn't roll off
but only pool
like still oceans
without need or sanity
till we hushed away
Gallifrey

Nine
Boogie in black coats
leather and shaven
rock the end of the world
to the end of wars
and the end of peace
burning away behind those eyes
like a killer
but prestigious in his cowardice

Ten
There is no Victim, only one
The Monolith
Standard of his own Monument
Unending and Victorious

A man with that Consequence
if only he could forget
those who were always the best of him

Eleven

Upon a shelf, doll like
tied up in bows
and sending himself in circles
finding the head at the tail
and eating the snake
opening up a grim fairy tale
with a hush for silence

Twelve

Eyebrows and Kidneys
    Renegade for the Masses
    Drifting off to the future
    without a pilot's license

Cushing

Away on Earth
with granddaughters
and repeat requiems
for the tin can menace
he is somehow familiar

half the hearts
but still ratcheting together
time and grace
with the ayre of
a mythical lord of time

Shalka Doctor

For just one alternating day
he shifted in and out
in loss of Gothic splendor
the mourners drag his slicked back hair
back to the mousse jar
and into the opera

Curse Doctor

Well, that was a lot of me
washed a way with a punchline
I wonder if I stick my hand in that socket--
well now I'm a woman
I'd been waiting for that.
Dalek bumps are cool
oh wait
no, those aren't those
But I'm onto adventures
with my hair down
my companion by my side
and a new set of possibilities
for the universe

Companions
Rose
Thornless and full of teeth
black wolf in sheep's clothing
    of the family
forged by non-linear propulsion
and a mist of years

Mickey
Beholden where the Tin Dog lie
she left you for an old man
watched and waiting
the least necessary man
        for all necessary time

Jack
I'm sure I'm sexy
he is to, and her
to you
and that horse, but lets not construe
your world as only hormones

because you weren't better as a coward
saving the earth
in a coat so hot for summer

waiting on hand
to play Doctor

Martha

You found a man who called him
self what you had earned
sweating in lab coats
as he smirked hi sway through decency
and yet he never noticed
that you were so much more
than a rebound

Donna

You were a Bride
but always so much more
than frilly gowns
made of unrolled wallpaper and cribs
you were songs
and note by note you became
symphonic
stretching across stars
and storming even soundless space
with cries of spaceman and earth-girl

till the score was erased
and once again wedding bells
struck out your incessant harmony

River
I have cried
but it has not removed the stain you left
when I had lost everything
I lost you before searching
putting your tombstone up
before I ever took your hand
and tangoed under orange skies
with your breath on my shoulder
and no idea

I had long ago
Become a widower

The Blue Book of River Song
Dear Diary,
today made the warden mad
I stole his books and made them read
he wasn't pleased to say the least,
nor that I wore his clothes to meet
him when he came to find me out
he said "No dinner!"
so I took his.
-River

Jail really isn't as bad as its said.

Dear Diary,
I went to study the Doctor's lore
and so, off to Metabelis four!
No, three, wrong planet
and whats more
I wouldn't recommend it more
than to send your worst enemy there.
-River

Dear Diary,
He took me to see the Beatles
and Paul McCartney hit on me
awkward date,
but seeing him awkward
well,
there's nothing wrong
with being hot
when you're clever and awkward
-River

Dear Diary,
Somehow I know
that there is someday
things go wrong
and he's seen that day
waiting for it's eventuality
as through I could go on forever

-River

Dear Diary,
If this book is me,
than let these pages be a reminder
that I flow like a song
and wind like a river
and no one can ever catch me
-Melody Pond

Wilf
There were wars
        and you suffered through
trapped on the soil
        when your telescope stared high
and the years went on
        but the stars can wait
with a patience
        untested
taking its time
        till fate
gives you the pain
        to knock at the door

Amy
Child eyed wonder

at a dollhouse time machine
warped with winnowing walls
and orphanhood

the kind of world that only outpours
in fair falls
drunk up to supplement
Fish Fingers and Custard
till you wake up
and the promises of imaginary friends
are as real as sleighbells
        on a lonely Christmas

Rory

tell me how you died?
Or have you lost count
when 2000 years you were
the representative of Rome
to all of England
a Human Doll
that makes the perfect husband

never faltering
you could wait for millenia
and she'd always be your
warm and plastic heart

Clara

Alaska in Space
and Barmaid Governess
to a flat in London
and unpaid breakfast times
you sever yourself
lost amidst the recipes
you become the cookbook

feeding the past,
with Souffles
lactose free
with unearned milk
serving 50 years
with French cuisine
From Gallifrey to Trenzalore

Monsters!

The Daleks

Such perfection was never so unseen
when blossoming hate unfurls your case
to wriggle your arms out at the sunlight
like infants
so overly excited
at your one word doctrine
shouted over the echos of your ancient footprints
lost in calcified forests and frozen beasts

you've come so far from that home

lost inside your own bodies
instruments of a cacophony
only you can exterminate

The Cybermen
We will survive
despite the dripping of our flesh
and the mortuary diligence of our skin
we fill the void of failed organs
with the squeezebox of chest plates
and re-routed power grids
muddling between our bodies
and a world seen through camera lenses
heard through speakers
felt though second nature
assimilating your iPods
into our very being

The Weeping Angels
the life you could have led tomorrow
is nowhere in 1894
and the kiss you leaned in for
is no one's in the march of the decades
brushing aside your windowsill
with frozen wings
your possibilities were endless
and now they are dinner

The Ice-Warriors
frozen away in red soil
riding the waves of the future
into parasites
you knock on your neighbor's door
with a hissing lisp hello
harrowing them
like vikings from space
martian invaders
just like the old serials said

The Silurians
under our feet in sarcophagi
slumbering for the day you can claim your thrones
unaware the monkeys wear their dunce crowns
while your heads drift on your pillows
dreaming of lands with dinosaurs
while those fleshy things with not a scale of grace
trod your lands like infants

The Silence #1

The Silence #2 (Eye-patch edition)

The gaps in your doctrine
have been doctored
like false memories
engineered childhood
to make mass attendance mandatory
in the struggling silence
of your shimmersilk memory
blinking away the last traces of your sight
as your last confession
we were ever here at all

Autons

Plastic men and other things
the whole world we live in
popped out of frames and molds
a ready made army
of underpaid labor

Slitheen
a gassy sort of profit
is to be made by all
by the skin of someone else's teeth, no less
hunting for the fall of all

The Master
Oh my Doctor,
aren't we a pair?
Couldn't we tromp the earth together
like gods of fairy tales?

But it wouldn't be so fun
without you to pounce
and lower my guard
so my plans could go south

You may be a nuisance
but by Kronos, a universe without you
scarcely bares thinking about

6 ESSAYS

Moffat, Gaiman, Davies, and Miles:
The Storytellers of Lost Dreams

A long time ago, Lawrence Miles penned a book called "Alien Bodies" that set out a rather unique vision of Doctor Who. He wasn't the first to do such a thing, nor would he be the last, but he would get fired for being hard to work with. In many ways this is a pity- after all his Doctor Who novels "Christmas on a Rational Planet", "Alien Bodies", "Interference Book One: Shock Tactic", and "Interference Book Two: The Hour of the Geek" present such a fully formed view of what he wants Doctor Who to be, its hard to not get taken in by it. That he went on to expand some of these ideas into their own book series was inevitable. That that book series never took off is fascinating. Lawrence Miles work on Doctor Who didn't vanish however, it got subsumed, as writers who saw the world as being a place just as magical, dark, virulent, and real took hold of the show. The pity isn't so much that Lawrence Miles' ideas never made it onto the screen, as that he never really got to write them himself. But more importantly, those ideas changed Doctor Who, and made it a darker and more magical show. He's one of a few writers who follow in the same trend for Doctor Who though, a trend to see Doctor

Who not as science fiction, but as its own mythology. A fairy tale about a mad man with a box, squids trapped in metal cases, and ancient lords of time who wait under the universe.

Lets get the obvious similarities out of the way: its very easy to make comparisons between the "War in Heaven" in Miles' books and the "Time War" of Russel T. Davies, so much so that reading Miles' books gives the same feel and tone for what the war is, even if the continuity details don't line up. When Davies writes about the Time War, it seems an impossible thing to imagine, with beautiful language about things like, "the Could Have Been King, and his army of Meanwhiles and Never-Weres", and the "Nightmare Child" inspire wonder. Imagining what on earth those things are is far better than any attempt to put them on screen, and wisely Davies (and later his following head writer Stephen Moffat) doesn't. This war consumed the TV show, and consumed the world outside of it to. The war that rages throughout all of history ended, but continues on in the Faction Paradox books. Yet, even there it is also over, as the comic book series of Faction Paradox is set after the end of the war as well.

That such a momentous thing as the Time War would happen off screen is monumental in itself. While we got to see a tidbit of the end of it in "the Day of the Doctor" such a glimpse could hardly by called representative of the whole, and such a glimpse does not an entire era of Doctor Who make. Without the Time War as a whole on screen, we are left with it as only tidbits, and those tidbits become even more important, as they make that time when Doctor Who wasn't on the air even more important. Suddenly, those years of not getting any more Doctor Who episodes become tangible in the type of stories that were supposed to fill them. No longer merely vacuous spaces, they becomes ghosts, haunted by the fleeting glimpses that Davies, Moffat, and indeed Miles as well have deigned to give us. What is left over is something we wish to grasp at, but which we can't, an eternal reminder that Doctor Who, no matter how much we may take issue with any given episode, series, or even show runner, is an institution that deserves to keep going long into the future, without the threat of another death where the show can churn in its comics, books, fan films, and audio dramas until it finally returns to the screen again.

Yet, all is not as it seems. Those comics, books, fan films, and audio dramas all helped shape the form of how Doctor Who returned to the screen. That in its first series when it came back in 2005 every single writer for the show had written a piece of prose Doctor Who fiction during the great hiatus speaks volumes, but that for most of them that fiction had all been written for the Seventh Doctor rather than the Eighth speaks quite a bit as well.

There were two runs of Doctor Who novels after the show was canceled in the 80's: the first was by Virgin, and were novels chronicling the continuing adventures of the Seventh Doctor, as well as extra adventures for the other Doctors One through Six. Exactly one novel was released by them for the Eighth Doctor, after which the line was turned over to the BBC's own publishing arm who began their own Eighth Doctor adventures line. This line is not as well regarded as the Virgin books like, and is generally treated as a step down in quality by fans, with the usual exception that briefly there was a writer named Lawrence Miles who came up with a radically new and fantastic direction for the Doctor to go in. His vision saw the Doctor finding out about his own death in a future war against an enemy whose identity was a secret, and who may have had no identity at all. The Time Lords of the future were fighting this enemy, which was less physical and more like an alternate form of history, and the Doctor began to be entangled in it through the efforts of a group of time traveling Vodou cultists called "Faction Paradox." This was a radically different route for the Doctor's story, and many became enraptured in it. Unfortunately he was apparently quite obnoxious to work with and got fired, and the vision for the series was over taken by Justin Richards, whose ideas about the nature of Doctor Who were interesting, and yet not quite as magical as Miles.

Richards thought he could strip Doctor Who down to its bones essentially, and removed the TARDIS and the Doctor's memories from the picture, for a brief time running a series of stories where a mysterious figure called the Doctor solved problems on Earth. It was a bare bones approach, one might go so far to say elegant if you're a fan of it, but it didn't capture audience's attentions as such. No, despite being kicked off the Doctor Who line, Miles' war simmered underneath it. The war itself, being a fight against history, being the fight for Doctor Who to remain in existence and return to the triumphant state it once was, lingered and waited to burst out.

Time passed. Moffat wrote sitcoms. Davies wrote dramas. Miles wrote elaborate and published Doctor Who fanfiction under the Faction Paradox banner (now its own book line). But we have yet to really introduce the other player in this piece, so lets move onto him.

Neil Gaiman was always an odd choice for Doctor Who, not because of his style of writing, but because he was relatively high profile author. Not so high profile that you see his novels on top of the New York Times Best Sellers list at the grocery store every day, but high profile enough someone outside of the circles of geeks might have heard of him, or at least seen a film based on one of his books.

Gaiman's most famous book, "American Gods," is a masterpiece of modern day mythology and urban fantasy. Supernatural beings and gods live among us like immigrants, sharing in our daily lives and gaining worship from us any way that they can. The book throws aside easy answers to its own questions, killing the villain only to have a different version of the villain appear later, a completely different god shaped from a completely different idea of that god. In it, our thoughts shape reality, and what we wish for and dream for can become tangible in ways that we can't actually see in front of our eyes. Wars of beliefs and ideas take physical form, and in many ways the gods are at the mercy of whether or not we chose to believe in them, or how.

Whats notable about this, is how similar "American Gods" is in this ideology to Miles' "This Town Will Never Let Us Go" of the Faction Paradox line. In that book, the war destroys buildings not because there is a tactical reason to, but because if they didn't no one would know there was a war on, and the characters from cereal boxes and snack food bags take physical shape, walking amongst the humans who eat them like Henry V before Agincourt. But Miles' view is much more pessimistic. Where "American Gods" shows those elements of the old world surviving, if not thriving, in the new world, "This Town" shows a world where the banality and horror of our existence can eventually shut off our ability to dream, our ability to form new thoughts. The deluge of corporate controlled media and rehashed ideas sculpted for the public ruins us.

That this is paralleled yet again in the first series of Doctor Who isn't surprising. Where the Doctor expects to find a whole new age of humanity in "the Long game" and "Bad Wolf" instead finds a society crippled to stagnation by its own media. While this doesn't take the form of aloof gods or beings that could be labeled as spiritual even in their corporate creation, this isn't quite as important as the underlying message, one also echoed in the villainous plots in "American Gods": we're all being manipulated, and really, no one is going to speak up about it, because the manipulation is pleasant and easy.

This is in many ways the ultimate Nightmare of men like Gaiman, Miles, Moffat, and Davies: the dissolution of creativity and dreams into monotony. When stories are your escape, what do you do when that escape has been hijacked and taken from you?

The answer of course, is to create new stories where its possible to create new ideas tangibly. Moffat, Gaiman, Miles, and Davies, all share in common this idea that individuals become empowered through the creation of stories, through treating their own lives as being more than simply ordinary, but mythic. Each writer has their own way of showing this idea, something which has led to much needless bitter banter about how one is empowering while the others aren't-- the truth is they all are, to different people in different situations. All four of them have crafted stories where we can become the stories we dream of. A girl in a shop can be the Bad Wolf, a milquetoast boyfriend can become the Last Centurion, a poor girl can become a Cousin in Faction Paradox to live in cities of smoke, a girl can live more lives than the Doctor, all throughout time to see all the places she ever dreamed of, a girl can escape the verbal abuse of her family and find safe places far away, a boy can find out he is the son of a god and take his place in the world, and a girl whose life is waiting can see the stars, and chose her own home with who she wants.

These adventures are not always easy, and they can end badly, but they have given Doctor Who and the author's other works this same feeling. While we may live in a tactile world, its one that is still magical, one where there are still dreams and fairy tales worth living out and trying for. You might not get there, but its worth it just just for the experience, but for the story. Every person becomes stories, and to live enough to tell your own, to craft them in whatever way you chose, now that is a life. You, and your fight against whatever monsters you encountered, are worthy of a voice.

I feel this is important, for while there are endless discussions about continuity, the way Doctor Who impacts people is more important than anything. The way it can uplift someone, and give them something to strive for, or believe in, some message to hold onto, that is what has kept it around all this time, and that's what will keep it going.

That simple dream, to live even our normal lives of work and chips in a way where good is done, and a story is worth telling about it, even a quiet one. There may not be Daleks and explosions, but when your story causes a dream, those will come on their own.

River Song's History

The only real blight on the intellect is the failure to imagine a situation where you are wrong." -No One, Yesterday, 2134

What exactly constitutes logic in fiction? After all, fiction is by its very name fictitious. One isn't going to get very far by trying to proclaim fiction to in fact be on par with science in terms of what is a logical plot thread, or "what is truth?" to quote Pilate. Nor will one get far attempting to make any sort of headway on deciding once and for all what a good story actually is. Stories are something outside of the realm of reason, not because they don't make sense, but because there are no explicit rules for stories. A story one person hates, can easily be another person's favorite, and neither of those people are wrong in the way they would be if they claimed 2+4 was 872, or that Neil Armstrong never walked on the moon. You can verify these things, but you cannot verify a story. Which leads to a quandary: when a story has multiple versions of it, how can you tell which ones are correct, or which ones are real?

Most readers will be familiar with the concept of "canon" an idea that there are certain elements of a story which "count" and there are others that are outside of the canon, and therefore are generally considered of less importance. The term comes from a religious usage, pertaining to which religious texts were accepted into religious doctrine, and which ones would be expunged from that canon and labeled "apocrypha." In Christianity, there is plenty of apocrypha; the gospels of Thomas, Judas, and Mary Magdalene for instance, as well as books one might consider Christian "spin off material" such as the Shepherd of Hermas, which doesn't feature the main characters of the Biblical New Testament, but is clearly meant to be in the same setting.

Framing this within religion may seem odd, but fans are a devoted lot, and there is a reason the term canon was chosen over other less holy words. These stories we have been told are important to us, they drive our lives, and the lessons we have learned from them can very often stick with us through our whole lives. One friend of mine noted that when I listed off my favorite quotations, they were all from either Jesus or the Doctor, and while I don't worship the Doctor, it would be stupid of me to deny he had a fundamental role in shaping who I am as a human being. In this way, the stories of the Doctor become more than just stories, fitting them into a logical system is practically pointless. That being said, I'm going to be doing it anyways!

However, this whole process becomes much trickier when you take into account things that could be, rather than things that are. The recent episodes "the Time of the Doctor" and "the Name of the Doctor" raise a very interesting question about River Song....

River: "Oh, there's one more thing..."
Doctor: "Isn't there always?"
River: "I was mentally linked with Clara. If she's really dead

then how can I still be here?"
Doctor: "Okay... How?
River: "Spoilers! Goodbye, sweetie."
(From "The Name of the Doctor" by Stephen Moffat)

That question is, is she really dead after all? The Doctor saved River into the Library, the largest database in the universe, a database that as we learned in the episode can take saved data and turn it back into people. While perhaps it would be more difficult to conjure up a new body for River Song, as the Library only saved her brain pattern... Why couldn't it work that out eventually? After all, she has a lot of time, and a huge computer to help.

River's appearance in "Name of the Doctor" gives us another possible hint of this, when the Doctor tells River that "She should have faded by now," implying that she has survived in the Library computer much longer than she should have. This all leads to the possibility that River survived, and the further possibility that she could be the character Tasha Lem from "the Time of the Doctor"

First appearance:
A Good Man Goes to War
River is a baby in the Silence's Kevorian chapter base at Demons Run.

The Impossible Astronaut/ The Day of the Moon
Little River is a child trapped in an orphanage or a wandering spacesuit in 1960's USA. She eventually regenerates into Mels in an alley in New York.

Lets Kill Hitler
River is Amy's childhood friend Mels, and regenerates into
the River we know well after Hitler kills her (Hitler is really
the worst.)

Closing Time
During the scene at the end of the episode, we see River
studying at the university after being saved by the Doctor in
Nazi Germany, where she is kidnapped by the Silence in
order to kill the Doctor, and put into the spacesuit again.

The Wedding of River Song
River meets the Doctor on the Beach at Lake Silencio, averts
killing him causing a massive time distortion, and eventually
does "kill him" after he marries her. The Doctor, however,
survives. River is put into the Stormcage prison, but she
won't stay in easily.

Minisode: First Night/Last Night
The Doctor goes to pick River up for their first night
together outside of Stormcage, and introduces her to the
concept of their Journals.

A Good Man Goes to War
River arrives at Demon's Run, and reveals to the Doctor,
Amy, and Rory who her parents are. That is, they are. Which
really is a surprise to everyone involved.

A Good Man Goes to War
River goes on a date with the Doctor ice skating, and while breaking into prison is confronted by Rory who asks for her help at Demon's run, but she tells him she cannot, as this is the day the Doctor learns who she is. Rory is understandably unhappy that his daughter wont help him find herself, but that will all get smoothed out.

The Impossible Astronaut/The Day of the Moon
The Doctor Invites River to watch his death at lake Silencio, proving that even people who come up with romantic iceskating dates under London Bridge with Stevie Wonder can botch a date every now and then, as well as setting off an adventure which leads to River chasing herself as a child and trying not to let on that she knows she is the child they are chasing.

The Pandorica Opens/The Big Bang
River breaks out of Stormcage and defaces a cliff to call the Doctor to Stonehenge, where they must solve the mystery of the Pandorica, and reboot the Universe. (After all, turning something off and back on again is what tech support would tell you to do).

Flesh and Stone/The Time of Angels
River goes on a mission for the Church of the Papal Mainframe to gain her freedom from Stormcage. While the mission is costly, it is successful.

The Wedding of River Song
River arrives in her parent's garden in the 21st century right after her mission on the Byzantium, and explains that the Doctor isn't really dead after all. At this point the Doctor erases all records of his own existence, meaning that technically the man River murdered never existed, so she gets let out of jail.

The Angels Take Manhattan
River says goodbye to her parents in 1930's New York, and writes a book that will be published with an afterword by her mother. She flies the Doctor's TARDIS out of the whole affair.

Minisode: The Rain Gods
The Doctor and River go on a date and accidentally wind up being led to be sacrificed to make rain. They get out of it when it rains.

Minisode: First Night/Last Night
River, on her last date with the Doctor before she dies, accidentally encounters the Doctor who has just picked her up for her first date with him outside of Stormcage.

Silence in the Library/Forest of the Dead
River meets the Doctor, the youngest she has ever met him, and he doesn't know her. She sacrifices herself to save him, and he repays her by saving her brain pattern in the Library computer for her to live on.

The Name of the Doctor
River lives on inside the Library computer, and helps the Doctor and Clara on their adventure, finally getting to say goodbye to a Doctor who knows her and love her, as she never could in the Library.

(?) Time of the Doctor (?)
Tasha Lem, who may or may not be River Song recreated by the Library computer, leads the church of the Papal Mainframe as its High Priestess, defending Trenzalore and the town of Christmas with the Doctor.

River's Timeline isn't strictly reverse-chronological from the Doctor's. While it is in large part, with several instances of there being two versions of River in a given episode (such as when she watches herself try to kill the Doctor at lake Silencio) being strictly reverse-chronological is in fact an impossibility. Some points on this timeline are somewhat conjecture, for instance the short "Rain Gods" could be placed at several places on this timeline with no real change in how well it fits into continuity, as it is a two minute scene with few ties to any particular plot threads. But generally, this order of events is solid.

However, that last entry on there brings up an interesting question: how much do we need to be sure is definitely canon in Doctor Who? After all, it could just be that Tasha Lem is a character with a lot of similarities to River song. Reading her character that way makes a certain amount of sense after all; she is the head of the church whose splinter group ends up making River into a weapon to begin with. That elements of her trickled down into River wouldn't be that surprising.

But if Tasha Lem is River Song, it adds a whole new element to her character. Its not just that she survives death, its that in many ways she becomes more important than the Doctor. While the Doctor runs around saving worlds where he lands, Tasha Lem runs a giant church able to send soldiers to deal with Weeping Angels, or protect an entire planet from being invaded and destroyed by a blockade that wishes to destroy any chance of Gallifrey returning. Tasha is able to provide not just safety for Trenzalore and Christmas, but countless other worlds. Tasha is in many ways what River might become if she lived to be older. River was always more skilled at flying the TARDIS than the Doctor, and more responsible in her own way. River was able to issue orders, command Romans, play tricks on people to get them to go her way, and break out of prison easily. She was clever, maybe more clever than the Doctor, and definitely better at planning. That River would be able to manage a whole Church/Military is hardly surprising at all.

But.... Does it matter if she is or not? If we are certain Tasha Lem is River, does that make her character more or less interesting? In many ways, leaving River's timeline ending on a question mark is the most appropriate way possible to end it. River may have had many questions about her life answered, but she is still always a mystery, and mysteries can drive our imaginations to wondrous places. So maybe she died in the Library, and is living on as an Echo till she fades out, or maybe she found a way out and is now the leader of a powerful religious organization. Either way, she lived quite the life, and its easy enough to imagine what she would say if you asked her if she was dead: Spoilers, Sweetie.

River's life is a mystery, and so is the nature of Doctor Who canon. There is no official pronouncement on what is and isn't canon, which is a very kind stance as with the paradoxes and rewriting of time travel, allows for technically all Doctor Who stories to be true, at least at one point before someone went back in time and changed it, or the Silence made everyone forget about it. If you want to believe only the TV show is canon, you can. If you want to believe the Peter Cushing movies are films that exist inside the Doctor Who Universe, Ian and Barbara having sold the rights for them, you can do that to. If you want to count in all of the Novels, Comics, Audio Dramas, and the Spin Off series like K-9, Faction Paradox, and Cyberon, you can do that to.

That's really the great thing about Doctor Who's canon, its whatever you want it to be, you can enjoy and work in anything you want to, and leave out what you don't like, and no one can stop you from making it any way you'd find enjoyable in your own mind.

The Doctor's Name

A long, long time ago, or maybe it was in our future, or the very moment you are reading this..... But no matter when, it was in another time, another world... A child was born we call "The Doctor". Now, this wasn't originally his name, we're fairly sure of that. Or maybe it was and all of the hubbub about his nomenclature is a massive and successful game of misdirection on his part... But the evidence would seem to point otherwise. Indeed, no question looms larger over the entirety of the series than that one simple question: Doctor Who? But if the Doctor's name isn't the Doctor, if its something else, hidden from all of us, what could that thing be, and why would he have hid it at all?

But first off, lets establish what we know. In "the Armageddon factor" the fourth Doctor meets his friend Drax from Gallifrey who mentions that he was called by the nickname "Theta Sigma" while in university there. In "the Name of the Doctor" the eleventh Doctor tells us that he chose the name the Doctor, and that it was a promise, further clarifying in "the Day of the Doctor" that the promise was to be "never cruel or cowardly," and to "never give up, never give in." We also have seen that the Doctor change his name when he finds himself moving away from that promise, and living by a different set of ideals. The first mention of this comes during the sixth Doctor's "Trial of a Timelord "story where we find the Doctor facing off against the Valeyard (which means "Doctor of the law") a future pseudo-incarnation of the Doctor that has shunned everything that made the Doctor the Doctor and become a true villain. The War Doctor later chooses to not call himself the Doctor for betraying the ideals of the Doctor during the time war, and the eleventh Doctor at one point says that if he crosses a moral line he will have to chose a new name because "I won't be the Doctor anymore." in "the Beast Below." After failing his companions Amy and Rory, he briefly does void himself of the name 'Doctor' and becomes "the Caretaker." Later, a character who may or may not be the Doctor at the end of "the Day of the Doctor" reveals themselves as "the Curator" a possible future incarnation of the Time Lord who runs an art gallery. The Tenth Doctor may also have briefly taken up the mantle of "Time Lord Victorious" at the end of "The Waters of Mars" showing that he was no longer bound by any rules. Finally, the Doctor uses the alias "John Smith" often when pretending to be a human, even using it as his name when he turns himself into a human in "Human Nature/The Family of Blood", and calls a mental projection of himself "the Dream Lord" in "Amy's choice".

From all of this, we can surmise that the Doctor's name is in fact impermanent, something that he wasn't always, and something that has changed before and might change again. So, we know that the Doctor's name is a promise, and that the promise changes. Therefore, it can be surmised that each of the Doctor's names says something about the promise he in making through appointing that as his name.

The Doctor of course implies that he is a healer, someone who makes people better, someone who doesn't stick around but hops in to fix a problem and leaves, perhaps popping back in to check up on things, but perhaps not. Its also an academic title, implying being a man of some learning, science, and wisdom. That the Doctor is so often portrayed as a scientist is no surprise then (and of course, in contrast, we have the Master, another academic title that implies control and dominance over other beings, the opposite of the Doctor's goals).

In contrast, the first alternate name we learn of, the Valeyard, is both archaic and obscure. It isn't a term that the average person could latch onto, and is definitely not a word that inspires any sense of hope upon hearing it. Consumed by rules and regulations, the Valeyard's main goal is to steal the Doctor's regenerations for himself, a paradoxical goal that entirely exists around knowing and bending arcane rules and regulations. The Valeyard is a perversion of the Doctor, and doesn't deserve of his name, just as the War Doctor rejects the Doctor's name during the Time War as he fights in it, feeling his actions during combat in the war made him not the Doctor anymore. (I prefer to call this incarnation "The Warrior" but as official sources call him the War Doctor, I shall do so as well in this essay.)

Etc, Etc... So the Doctor hasn't been the Doctor his entire life. But what the Doctor's birth name is must have incredible meaning in some way, or at least one that he doesn't want anyone to know about, or perhaps simply can't let anyone know about. So here comes the real question: why doesn't the Doctor want anyone to know his real name? While we can't know for certain, here are a few possibilities:

1. The Doctor's name itself is imbued with mystical properties. For instance, knowing the Doctor's real name might give a person power over him in some way. In many traditions, learning the name of a supernatural being enables a person to have power over that being, often to control it or exorcise it. Here the Doctor avoids giving his name out because it is dangerous for any Time Lord to, it would be like giving someone the key to your house, your car, and your bank account information. While some people might be trusted with it, like River Song, in general people knowing would be hugely dangerous.

2. The Doctor's name is the key to bringing back Gallifrey, and while he and the Time Lords didn't know specifically why at first, they did know that his name was dangerous for some reason. After all, if your name can unlock gate to let an entire planet back into existence that was waging a war throughout all of time, it might be possible that rumors of that danger spread to the Doctor even before the war was begun, or he even knew that the war was a possibility. This is a very paradoxical solution, but that is the nature of time travel anyways.

In this eventuality, the Doctor has always been haunted by his name. In the same way the Master was haunted by the constant drumming in his head the Time Lords placed in his mind in order to link him to the Time War ("The End of Time"), The Doctor, like the Master, has always been running, and linking his birth name to the Time War, making it the code to pull Gallifrey out, doesn't seem out of character for the heavily manipulative and meddling

High Council of Gallifrey during the war.

By this reading, the Doctor running away from Gallifrey would be only natural, as would replacing his name with something else. After all, he would have always been "that" child, the one with the dangerous name, the name no one was supposed to say. The Time Lords might have even placed bans on people saying the Doctor's name, leaving him the victim of the sort of alienation that can befall a child who is different from the others. By becoming the Doctor, he escapes from all of that, by stealing a TARDIS and running away, he becomes his own Time Lord, undefined by the rule and stereotypes placed around him. The name "the Doctor" becomes his liberation, defining himself away from the unspeakable name.

3. The Doctor is a figure from Gallifrey's history, and his name would reveal some deep secret about him. In the serial "The Brain of Morbius" there is a sequence which possibly shows other regenerations of the Doctor before the First Doctor. The explanations for this have been many: Marc Platt wrote in his novel "Lungbarrow" that the Doctor was in fact the pseudo-reincarnation of the Time Lord known as "the Other" who helped Rassilon and Omega found Time Lord civilization itself. Others have speculated that the Doctor was someone else important on Gallifrey, perhaps a revolutionary or mad scientist, who reformed and secured a new identity (and new regeneration cycle) for himself to start over.
 In this case, the Doctor hiding his identity is truly

paramount, as anyone who learned that he was this important figure would want to glean the secrets of that life from him. While there are problems with this theory, namely that for the Doctor to be the Other in the way Marc Platt intended, the Doctor would have to have not been born but "woven" on the genetic Looms of Gallifrey from leftover material there. That the Doctor had a cradle ("a Good Man Goes to War"), a Mother and Father ("the TV Movie"), and a childhood in general seem to contradict this. Having had a previous regeneration cycle is problematic as well, what with how many people have gone into the Doctor's mind.

But that doesn't entirely rule it out. Morbius himself has a lot of trouble getting that far into the Doctor's head, a ridiculous amount, and it ends up being far too much for him. Another bit that could support this, is when Rory Williams talks about how his memories of being a Roman are behind a door in his head, one that he often kept closed. If the Doctor had such a door, and kept it locked, perhaps people going into the Doctor's mind might simply never find it or be able to get through. Perhaps the Doctor has closed the door on that past life himself to keep it from cropping up, by hiding the memories of it even from himself.

This explanation gives the greatest weight to the Doctor's real name; whatever it is, it is not just important, it is of cosmic important. Stars could die by its mere mention, and the universe shift slightly towards some new destiny.

4. The Doctor's name is just really dumb. While this isn't the most romantic or nifty explanation, if the Doctor had some very embarrassing Gallifreyan name, one that was considered improper in some way, or just awkward (for instance, if his name were Liqonqwueeataweekweekgranblak, or Cherry Gumball Hat) the Doctor might not like saying it, or anyone else knowing it. This explanation isn't terribly interesting from a canon perspective, but deserves to be mentioned all the same.

5. Saying any Time Lord's name is simply taboo or bad manners, unless they achieve great social rank. While it can be surmised that some Time Lords like Rassilon go by their birth names, one interesting possibility is that for Time Lords going by one's birth name is not a right, but a privilege. For example, in this scenario, the Doctor would have chosen the name the Doctor, earned the right to be called "Theta Sigma" at University, but never earned the right to go by his birth name do to never achieving anything notable, or simply because he went renegade stole a TARDIS and ran off. He might have gotten to the point where his name was right to reveal, but never did. The only problem with this theory is that the Doctor became the President of Gallifrey, which seems pretty important, really, as achievements go. Then again, he wasn't President for that long, and shirked his duties as quickly as he possibly could.

6. The Doctor's name reveals a secret not about himself, but about the nature of all Time Lords. In this scenario, all Time Lords hide their names. What their real names are is something deeply secret, something that would cause a huge stir if people did know it. Perhaps each Time Lord is a god from our mythology, or maybe even the mythology of every world. Maybe each Time Lord is a fundamental piece of the Universe, not just a creature of the universe, but a function of it, performing their roles like integral parts of its body, the white blood cells of its time stream. In this case, learning the name of the Doctor wouldn't so much be dangerous as overwhelming, to most beings it might overload their brains the same way that Donna Noble's brain couldn't handle the Doctor's mind in "Journey's End". Saying the name would be like saying the meaning of a part of the universe in such a deep and complete way that it would be impossible to fully comprehend. River could learn it because she was sort of a Time Lord, and Clara lost her memory of learning it in "Voyage to the Centre of the TARDIS", and never had it sit around in her head long enough for it to over load her (remember that it took Donna some time to be overwhelmed by what she learned). The Doctor has to keep his name secret not just for his own safety, but everyone around him's. Learning the name of a Time Lord could be deadly.

The show itself will probably never answer this question firmly. The only reason it was answered in "Lungbarrow" was because it was the end of the Doctor Who book's line at the time, and it being the end, they figured there was nothing to lose by doing a story like that. In many ways, answering the question, "Doctor Who?" is something you can only do in a "last" Doctor Who story. Even then, the decades of build up to the question would make any answer you can give rather anti-climactic to many fans. However, I'm glad the question is there, because asking who the Doctor is is part of the fun of the show. There are so many possibilities about his origins, what originally caused him to chose the name "the Doctor" with all its many connotations and extra meanings, and why he never says his original name that to narrow it down to just one seems almost a tragedy for the minds of fans. When I was a child, I used to wonder who the Doctor was, and I still do. Its something I think every fan should have the chance to do.

But the Doctor's name as just "the Doctor" is no less important. Its a name that means in itself that we are cared for, its a name that gives hope. The promise of Doctor Who as a show, that even in the darkest most dangerous times there is a solution out there that doesn't need to happen with slaughter, that you can win by being clever and having friends, is a promise that I hold close to my heart. Its a promise that in many ways, makes knowing the Doctor's "real" name pointless. Because for all the semantics of it, he chose the name the Doctor, and we love the man that uses that name and everything it stands for.

So cheers to the Doctor.

...Wait which Doctor?

Doctor... Who?

Romana is the Best Companion

On Spinoffs, Timelords, and why there can only be one Doctor.

If you have every watched the Doctor Who spinoffs Torchwood and the Sarah Jane Adventures (or, really, even K-9 and company or Disney's illegitimate "K-9" show) there is a common question you can tell the writers asking themselves over and over: This show is a spinoff of Doctor Who, so how can we make it like Doctor Who without the Doctor? The answer is of course a rather cheery one; the Doctor's companions become sort of mini-Doctors when the leave, taking the lessons they learned from the Doctor and starting their own hodgepodge teams of day-savers. And yet, these spinoffs often lead to some serious quandaries about why the Doctor didn't step in to save the day (especially in a longer running story like "Children of Earth" or "Miracle Day") and either have to let their protagonists deal with smaller scale problems, or fail miserably in comparison to the Doctor. Indeed, Torchwood could easily be retitled, "The Tragedy of Jack Harkness: The Doctor who couldn't", and becomes a much more interesting show when Jack's methods are compared to the Doctor. So, comparing companion's activities to the Doctor is common, and they are usually shown to fall somewhat short, except one, except Romana.

While I personally hope for a female Doctor to take the helm of the TARDIS someday, there is a line of fan desire to see the companion become like the Doctor in all but name. However, as a long term fan of the show I've seen that storyline already done, and it was wonderful. This is the story of Romana: the companion that could.

Romana is one of only two companions on Doctor Who who were also Time Lords, the only other one being the Doctor's granddaughter Susan. She was played by two actresses (as she regenerates during her tenure) the late Mary Tamm and Lala Ward, who was briefly married to co-star Tom Baker. Yes, co-star. While Romana was on the Tardis, her character was just as capable as the Doctor, outwitting foes, and acting like an equal rather than a damsel in distress. Slowly, she becomes the Doctor, if the Doctor was a refined but spunky woman, completely taking over for the Doctor in one Notable serial (the Horns of Nimron) until finally she comes to the realization that as much as she likes traveling with the Doctor, she wants to do what the Doctor does, and as long as she is travelling with him, she will never exceed his greatness, only meet it. But the Doctor is a universal force, whether he wants to be or not, he lives in a Blue Box that will take him to anywhere there is trouble, in any time or place. There isn't any room for more than one Doctor in our universe, you can't have two men who can be anywhere and everywhere saving the day, or the show isn't Doctor who anymore.

This is the Narrative problem of Torchwood, and to a lesser extent the Sarah Jane Adventures. If there is a problem with aliens, it's hard to not think of Sarah Jane or Jack Harkness as being the Doctor's B-team, because let's be frank, they are. If there was no more Torchwood, and no more stories were told about the Torchwood team ever, in the end it is a safe assumption that the universe would still be safe. This isn't an insult to the team, or the show, but it's a simple fact of the narrative logic of the series, one sadly proved by the passing of Elizabeth Sladen, star of the Sarah Jane Adventures, which meant that there would be no more adventures about how she saved the earth. Yet, as we see on Doctor Who every week, the Earth goes on, and while SJA, and TW both have devoted fanbases and creative writing teams, in the end they are both dependent on the existence of the Doctor.

So what is Romana's solution, how can she fulfill her true potential and not simply yank at the Doctor's coattails? Her solution is simple:

She finds another universe.

I can't state enough what a shock that moment was, when Romana tells the Doctor she isn't coming with him, and is staying in a different universe without him, and what a powerful moment it still is. Go watch "Warrior's Gate" the serial it happens in, it's really worth watching.

If the Doctor is so big that no one can equal him in his own reality, then the only solution is to be the Doctor somewhere he can't be. While sadly there was never any Romana spin off, I still like to imagine that there are countless untold stories of Romana's adventures, a new Doctor for a new universe, travelling in her own Tardis, and saving the day. The fact that we never see her again, that she never comes back to say she misses the Doctor, or secretly loves him, or anything silly like that only goes to strengthen that moment. If she had a reunion with the Doctor, the magic would be dead. The magic lies in her absence, the way the show refused to denigrate her character to having wasted away under unfulfilled love the way Sarah Jane was disempowered in "School Reunion".

But there will never be another Romana, the Doctor's companions have all been human so far in the new series, there are no Time Ladies left to take up his mantle, and a human has only one short life to live. Not to mention they wouldn't have their own Tardis, and without a Tardis, you aren't a Doctor at all. Which does of course, hedge on the clear error earlier in this paragraph, "what about Jenny?" you may say, "she is alive, as is River Song!" yes, but both are trapped within the timeline of Doctor Who. River will only ever appear on episodes of Doctor Who, as will Jenny, and neither of them will be able to escape from the fact that until they appear again on screen, no actions they take are affecting the narrative of the show. Like the children in "silence in the library", when we close our eyes they seek to exist, fully dependent on the narrative of the mad man in a box to rescue them to existence.

As much as I want to see Romana again, she is better gone, better never to see the Doctor again, because as soon as she re-enters our reality, she is entering the Doctor's reality, the Doctor's rules, his playground. And that would be a real shame. She is free now, she has left the confines of the show to a place the Doctor cannot go, and in her Tardis she will never be constrained by the Doctor, because she isn't part of his story anymore.

It's easy to just talk about women's empowerment without really meaning it, and there are plenty of forced moments of it in media, designed to elicit jubilant responses from the female part of the audience without actually doing anything meaningful, so its very rare that one is this real, and this honest. So, here's my sales pitch as a BBC DVD salesman: Warrior's Gate is the most legitimate piece of female empowerment in Doctor Who history. Also, it's got visuals that remind me a lot of the movie "Labyrinth". You should watch it.

The Doctor has had plenty of spunky, feisty, smart, and strong women as his companions, but only one was ever his equal. Only one was Romana.

Only one was her own story, in the end.

The SFX of Doctor Who
by Andrew Gilbertson

The special effects in Doctor Who have often been assessed as 'not so special.' Along with the shaky sets and cheap costumes, this analysis contributes to a time-worn cliché that has endured in popular culture nearly as long as Tom Baker's scarf or Peter Davison's celery. And certainly, when viewed alongside the contemporary (and budget-breaking) effects of a program like Star Trek, there does seem to be a great divide. The effects of Doctor Who are a product of their time, and their available BBC budget, just as they remain on the show today. But to dismiss those effects as uniformly subpar is to do a great disservice to the long, storied, and often-innovative history of special effects on Doctor Who.

Even from the beginning, the effects of Doctor Who were based on innovation on an extremely limited budget. The 'howlaround' techniques that comprise the unique and iconic opening sequence, based on the static resulting from a camera pointing at its own monitor (the 'infinite tunnel' technique that any kid who's hooked up a camcorder to TV or computer has played with), was invented by the camera operator for Doctor Who as a method of providing something never before seen on TV... with the limited resources at his disposal. And nearly a decade later, the time-tunnel credits that ended Jon Pertwee's era and comprised the majority of Tom Baker's were performed with the pioneering 'slit scan' technique developed for the iconic stargate sequences in 2001: A Space Odyssey... and yet, in keeping with Doctor Who's budget-consciousness, the subjects of the photography were stretched plastic grocery bags. The improvisational, the innovative, and the inexpensive, all at once.

This is not to say that every effect in Doctor Who was a pioneering effort. The limited 'almost-live' filming techniques of the early shows, as well as the aforementioned budgeted, necessitated extremely simple effects at times; glows and flashes and other bright spots, superimposed live, along with the occasional model-work. Both are on display in the second serial, 'The Daleks'- a tumbling piece of sculpture looks not half-bad, while the bright flash of energy when the Doctor shorts out the Daleks' static electricity control box is par for the course of the time, and not a terribly impressive effect by modern standards.

60s Doctor Who would continue in much the same mode; while models became more prevalent and more impressive in Troughton's run, animation and effects overlays remained fairly primitive. The former culminated in examples like the impressive TARDIS breakup and console in the void from the Mind Robber (a common critique being that the model Zoe's arms are too long on the miniature; fortunately, no male viewer, at least, was focused on her arms for this scene), the excellent Monoid statue in The Ark, and the smooth work showcased in what little survives of The Space Pirates. The latter is better evidenced in unfortunately-static shots like the hypnotic rays of the same

Mind Robber, and the average Cyberman lightning beam...
graphical overlays that stuck with the camera, even when
the shot panned- as a result, the simple animations and
graphics tended not to remain synched to their point of
origins, drifting off course as the camera shot did, remaining
fixed to its center instead of their onscreen sources.

Where the effects of this era really shine, however, are
the live construction and creature effects. Even as the
bluescreening in Planet of the Giants will win no awards, the
giant fly is impressively constructed and moves with
extreme realism and complexity, blowing away all
comparators. Where the Zarbi and 'flying' Menoptra of The
Web Planet fail to wow, the Animus tendrils and their
interaction with the main cast do. Even where the
occasional effect in The Daleks remains a little lackluster,
the fossilized dog certainly isn't. Scale models intended to
convey a certain size (such as the opening materialization in
The Keys Of Marinus, or the Mechanoids in the miniature
city from 'The Chase') may not always convince that they
are more than an inch tall, but the on-set, full-size models
are superb. The alien delegates (including my favorite, who
looks like the Fantastic Four's 'The Thing') from The Dalek
Cutaway impressive, even through blurry telesnaps. And say
what you will about he wobbly spikes of 'The Screaming
Jungle'- when those vines begin to smash through the walls,
accompanied by the sound and fury of the audio
department (which deserves its own essay), it's hard not to
be carried along by the effective on-set action.

The most difficult element of judging the early 60s

effects is the lost nature of many of them. The death of Katarina (the first *real* companion death!) looks impressive in fan reconstructions... did it look the same when it first aired? The Myth-makers (an underrated and hilarious classic) promises impressive Trojan Horse model work, but did it truly deliver? The rapid aging climax of The Daleks Master Plan wows with ambition and scale in description... but how did it *look*?

It's hard to say- but judging on the surprisingly impressive model and splitscreen work in the recently-recovered Enemy of the World, and the surprisingly sublime final shot of the serial, I'm tempted to say that the effects of the 60s, especially many of the lost Dalek stories, may have excelled beyond the credit we give them.

If this section of the essay comes off as a bit of a love-letter to 60s Who, chalk it up to author bias; even so, it would be remiss not to mention a few other effects standouts that give lie to the 'cheap effects' myth- namely the psychedelic and impressive Ice Warrior demises from The Seeds of Death, masterpieces of editing and photo negativity (which had also been used to give the Daleks their iconic weaponry, ironically abandoned in the higher-budget Cushing films as it was too expensive to reproduce on film instead of video tape), the transformation sequences in the oft-underrated Faceless Ones, the tomb miniature in Tomb of the Cybermen, the impressively minimalist practical work of the monster from Fury From The Deep (as well as those frightening open-mouthed moments from Mr. Oak and Mr. Quill, which deserve mention as special effects in and of themselves!), numerous techniques from the Mind Robber (most especially the Medusa, who has to be the conceptual and stylistic brother to the modern Weeping Angels) and other effects that we suspect of greatness, but cannot prove. Such unknown hopefuls exist in the opening and final chapters of the Wheel In Space, the closing part of Evil of the Daleks, and the mutant creatures and Dalek factory in Power of the Daleks. It is my greatest hope that we will someday be able to see for certain.

This brings us to 70s Doctor Who, which was, in many ways, the age of CSO. 'greenscreen' techniques (utilizing a different methodology, but most-closely comparable to that better known effect) allowed the scope of the show to expand enormously- from environments like the cave in The Mutants and the spacecraft in The Ambassadors Of Death, to the existence of pupeteered monsters such as the doll from Terror of the Autons, maggots in The Green Death, giant Cybermats from Revenge of the Cybermen, Omega's scout from The Three Doctors, and even a cybernetic parrot and a pair of noncorporeal judges for the Key To Time series. Neither the impressive ravaged-Earth ending of Inferno, part 6, nor the innovative Forbidden Planet-inspired monster from Planet of Evil, would have been possible without the extreme advances in this area of effects, probably the strongest point of the decade. The improvement in the effect is marked; just look at the difference between the static-fringe filled spaceship interior of Ambassadors of Death and the very rough Brigadier-with-a-flare shot from Invasion of the Dinosaurs, and compare it with the smooth otherworldliness of Warrior's Gate. Zygon spaceships, Omega's missing self... most of the memorable effects from this era came from CSO technology.

The 70s transcended mere superimposition, however; this was, in many ways, the most experimental decade of special effects work in Doctor Who. In addition to animated work (lightning bolts that kept their marks in Planet of the Spiders, the simple-but-omnipresent red ray of K-9's laser beam), the show dabbled in stop-motion (in the Seeds of Doom, impressively- just as it had once before in The Mind Robber- and less-successfully in Terror of the Zygons), and effects made possible by the light-reflective scotchlite (the same material that gave Kryptonians glowing clothes and Superman such crisp rear-screen projection in Superman: The Movie, and the average highway street-sign its distinct visibility), such as the titular Green Death, and the glowing eyes from Planet of Evil.

At the same time, the previously-improving model work that had been a 60s high point began to fall off. Shots of the TARDIS spinning through space continued to look fairly cheap, and miniatures (like the Dalek army in Planet of the Daleks) continued not to impress. Focus on CSO left model-work technology at a 60s-level throughout much of the early 70s, and the practical monster effects (minus a few impressive exceptions, such as the tentacles in Day of the Daleks and the fan-favorite Zygon costumes) tended not to impress. Much more of it, sadly, feel into the realms of out-of-focus silver bird-man Kronos and the unfortunate Nimon.

Again, the CSO advance seemed to have its costs, and what had been the strong-suit of the previous decade was left to flounder as other areas were improved upon instead.

Other standouts include the hand and eye effects of The Hand Of Fear, the Krypton-esque landscapes of The Deadly Assassin, the Sand Miner shots from Robots of Death, some of the model-work in Underworld, and a few of the mixed-bag from the over-rated City of Death.

And hey, the Dalek photo-negative effects finally became constrained to a zone around their victims instead of the whole screen.

There is some question as to whether the Krargs of Shada, with their CSO technique, would have looked as good in the original as reconstructions have painted them, much less how the multi-TARDIS vortex-chase would have come off... but it is safe to say that, while effects took a bit of a dip in the unfortunately short-changed Leela era, by the transition into the 80s and Baker's last year, things had picked up tremendously.

The 80s saw a return to form for Doctor Who. Model-work surged ahead once more, led by the truly astounding opening shot of Trial Of A Time Lord (a personal vote for best effects shot of all time in Doctor Who) and the soft-focused, ethereal city-ship of Dragonfire. CSO use fell off, while matte and practical model-work remained strong, but not far-advanced from their 70s counterparts... a solid middle-of-the-road. Practical, onset creature effects never quite recovered their previous heights, either, and it's primarily model-work and cinematography that carry Doctor Who through its final era.

CSO gets a few final days of glory in Meglos, Warrior's Gate, and Four To Doomsday, while Resurrection of the Daleks, Enlightenment, and the president's demise in Caves of Androzani kick off an era of much-improved miniature work.

Season 23, and Doctor Who's trial-probation, ironically, lead the show into a new period of almost filmic quality, saving its best for last; though there are exceptions (Terror of the Vervoids, The Happiness Patrol), this final era of the show presents a slick face, whatever one may think of the story quality. Again, innovative (and less 'cheap') techniques are embraced in the use of early CGI (which turns in a nifty opening title sequence, but thankfully isn't kept around for in-show effects beyond the teaser for Time And The Rani, which looks like a trial run for The Infinite Quest), time-lapse effects (such as the villain's demise in Dragonfire, 'borrowed' out of ILM's recent catalog for the villains of Raiders of the Lost Ark- as much from Dragonfire was 'borrowed'), and... whatever the heck that psychedelic ball of ludicrous death was- once again, in Time and the Rani. Practical pyrotechnic and model-work brings a new scale to the show in scenes such as the climax of Silver Nemesis, and the Dalek battles in Remembrance of the Daleks, and the spectacles (intermittently-mixed with less stellar effects) that cap off The Greatest Show In The Galaxy.

As the show came to a close, Daleks got beams and photo-negative outlines, the glowing animation-effects of

Light from Ghost Light dazzled, and the climactic scenes of an apocalypse on the planet of the Cheetah people (now there's a sentence you don't see every day) certainly proved that, whatever else was happening with the show, the production values were only continuing to improve.

Effects-wise, classic Doctor Who went out on a high-note.

The TV movie brought Doctor Who entirely into the CGI era, where it has dwelled ever since; slick, grand, sometimes-cartoonish, and very uniform in technique (barring moments, like Aliens of London, where traditional model-work was retained). Since, there has been far less variation in the effects of the show- merely a steady progression of improving CGI. Standards and appearances have remained largely uniform, which is both good, and perhaps, a little bad. We're always guaranteed a certain level of quality- but without the level of experimentation we once had, a general sameness reigns... and it is far more rare to find a true stand-out effect to wow and impress an increasingly effects-jaded audience anymore.

Certainly, looking back over the scope of Doctor Who's impressive 50 years, it is possible to support the 'poor special effects' stigma when focusing solely on the weakest aspect of each era's productions- but this ignores both the context of the available budget, and the numerous other areas in the show where production excelled past limitations, delivered solid effects- especially in the area of CSO puppetry- not being seen anywhere else on TV, and even managed to innovate. Even in an era of CGI and larger budgets, not every effect has been a success.

Over the long history of Doctor Who, there is a clear pattern of fluctuating strengths and weaknesses... but a continual striving for maximization of potential is evident through all of them. For every Time-Flight bubble-cocoon, there's an opening shot of The Mysterious Planet. For every Invasion of the Dinosaurs (come on, you guys, it wasn't *that* bad- the brontosaurus actually had a *fantastic* paint job), there's a Deadly Assassin. And more importantly, there are dozens of unsung heroes every week, striving behind the scenes with a shoestring budget to make every effect that they put on-screen the best that it could be. To the eyes of this author, at least, they succeeded in that- against overwhelming odds- far more often than they failed.

The next time you're watching classic Doctor Who, try looking out for what impresses you as opposed to the more infamous laugh-out-loud failures, and you may be surprised just how many solid, cinematic, and even astounding vistas have slipped your notice... simply because they were so well-executed as to call no attention to themselves, but solely supported the vision of the story.

Dalek History
by Andrew Gilbertson

In many ways, the history of the Daleks- complex and open to interpretation as it is- is not about history at all. Instead, it's about continuity. Continuity has always been notoriously hard to define in Doctor Who... and there's a partial reason for that. After all, this is a show about Time Travel.

Take the Back to the Future movies as an example. Marty McFly has experiences with his wimpy family and dominant Biff in 1985, then travels back to 1955. When he returns, the 1985 he knew is gone. He still remembers it, having occurred in his subjective past- but objectively, the events he remembered no longer exist in the altered timeline; at least, not in the same way. The same effect is doubtles occurring for the Doctor constantly, and on a much larger scale- adventures that we see him have being wiped from existence in all but his memory, erased by changes wrought by adventures further in the past.

This same phenomenon is key to the history of the Daleks.

Indeed, it is a subject that I became interested due to its apparent contradictory nature after watching 'Planet of the Daleks'. The Dalek Invasion of Earth was set explicitly in the 2170s, and the Doctor noted that the events of 'The Daleks' happened 'a million years later,' suggesting that it took place around the year 1,002,170 AD or so- give or take a few centuries. 'Planet of the Daleks' is set in 2540 AD- about

999,630 years *earlier*- yet those events are not only in the *past* of this story, they're ancient enough to have become legend, and for the Thals to have developed from hunter/gatherers in the jungle to a spacefaring race. Plus, the Daleks, somehow *survived* being utterly wiped out at the end of 'The Daleks' to show up in 'Planet'!

This is emblematic of the contradictory nature of Dalek stories, throughout both the old and new series. However, Doctor Who fans have never been daunted by a good challenge, and with a little bit of logic, this history- or, more accurately considering the revisionist nature of time travel, 'histories'- of the Daleks begins to fall into place. Other sources, including novelizations, have provided their own retcons, timelines, and versions of Dalek history. Leaving those aside- as entirely viable alternatives to what I propose- and going solely off of onscreen evidence, this is an analysis on how the history of the Dalek race seems to fit together. It is neither authoritative, nor conclusive... but I'd like to think it's logical.

A notable caveat: this essay assumes that the problem faced in 'Time of the Doctor' is a perennial Dalek issue; with the Daleks as ultimate conquerors, and the incredible potential for conquest through time travel (strike down your enemies before they become strong!) it is assumed that the acquisition of time travel comes late in the game in any Dalek timeline, and that this technology, once gained, will not be lost again. The Genie won't go back in the bottle, so to speak- once the Daleks gain time travel, it's game over... one way, or another.

So, let's start at the beginning. Early on, the Daleks are created by the mad scientist Davros in the midst of a nuclear war between the Dals and the Thals. (as we see an alternate version of in 'Genesis of the Daleks.') We know that this story occurs 500 years before 'The Daleks,' so, based on our conjectural dates below, we'll give this event- the origin of the Daleks- a purely theoretical timing of the mid-1700s, Earth-time. The date isn't truly important, in the end- regardless of when, this foundational event kicks off what we will call the 'First Timeline' of Dalek history.

In this version of Genesis of the Daleks, the Doctor is not present. Davros is exterminated, and while the Thal/muto alliance still cave in the bunker, it is not until a number of fully-finalized Daleks have escaped; only a contingent of their force is buried. The escaped Daleks then wage a brutal and terrible war against the Thals, literally blasting them back to the stone age- and then take to space to become a vast, mighty empire.

Meanwhile, the part-cannibalizing, limited Daleks buried in the bunker, left to their own devices, eventually escape it far behind their kin- emerging on a dead world and setting up shop in the old, abandoned city.

While the 'alpha' Daleks are out becoming the scourge of the stars, decimating worlds and becoming a feared intergalactic empire, these lesser 'beta' units create a rudimentary, less advanced civilization, powering themselves via static electricity. These inbred, hillbilly units become both degenerated by and addicted to the rampant radiation- especially those left behind in the old city. A few leave soon enough, in their rickety saucers, to at least remain away from the radiation for a time.

These 'beta' marauders seek out a power-base from which to launch a conquest of the galaxy, knowing that the primitive, run-down Skaro offers few resources. They fix on Earth, a planet ideal to be converted into a mobile battlestation due to its unique construction (something that has already been demonstrated in proof of concept, unbeknownst to them, by the twin-planet Mondas). Lacking the numbers or technology for a direct assault, this handful of saucer launch a sneaky scavenger attack, softening up their target with plague, conquering the Earth in 2164... by now, a good five-hundred years after their initial entombing setback.

Setbacks remain their lot in life, however, as the Doctor comes to the Earth a decade later, in the company of his granddaughter and a pair of schoolteachers. This is the Daleks' first chronological encounter with the Doctor- but one that leaves no survivors. This leaves the home vanguard of 'beta units' behind on Skaro blissfully unaware of the Time Lord as he arrives for his second chronological encounter (his subjective first) with their race- uniting with the Thals to end this bumpkin branch of the Dalek race. In the aftermath, he believes- as he tells Jo Grant- that he's destroyed them for good. (In the process, the First Doctor- a hot-headed, brash, arrogant youngster at only 450 years old- drastically overestimates the dates, assuming 1,000,000+ AD when he's really in the late 22nd century. If he didn't bother to do more than glance at the radiation counter, why should he have noted the accurate date?).

He's right, in that the pathetic beta-Daleks have been utterly obliterated. But the 'Alpha' Daleks, the originals, have forged a terrible and deadly empire in the last half-millennia. Their forces spread across the galaxy like a plague- which remains one of their key tactics of conquest, an idea that they and the betas both came to... a logical outgrowth of their belief in the genetic inferiority of other species. Of course physically impure races would be susceptible to attacks on their 'weaker' biologies, in the minds of the Daleks.

Undoubtedly, this period of history sees a number of offscreen encounters with the Doctor; by the time that we next see the Daleks on the planet Exxilon, they're using TARDISes for target practice, with a well-ingrained hatred of the Doctor. This world is just one of their many defeats during an expansionist period that brings them routinely into conflict with Earth. This reign of terror continues (largely unchronicled by the show) until the year 2540, where the Daleks (now employing Ogron mercenaries to carry out their plans while their own manpower remains dedicated to the front lines, a partnership that will last for centuries) mass an ultimate invasion force on Spiridon, planning to use invisibility as a secret weapon to conquer Earth once and for all.

The Thals, meanwhile, have reverse-engineered beta-Dalek technology and become a spacegoing race in the preceding 300 years (a rapid development due to the inherited tech). The story of the Doctor has become a part of their mythology in that time, a half-remembered artifact of their near-extinction time. Based on Skaro, the Thals now spend their days taking the fight to the Dalek Empire. And, after the events of 'Planet of the Daleks,' that empire is dealt a major setback, with its massive invasion force entombed.

Stymied by the forces of Earth and Skaro, the Daleks switch tactics, initiating research on a new branch of warfare… one that will spell the beginning of their end.

Time travel.

In the mean time, they continue to be known as a scourge of the galaxy- eventually retaking Skaro from the Thals (where they learn, with surprise, of the stunted legacy of the beta Daleks). One of their three foes has been eliminated by this point in history, perhaps around the 30th century- but two great foes remain, persistently stymieing the Daleks.

Eventually, after defeats and Earth-empire stalemates that last well past the 39th century, thousands of years of frustrated conflict, the Daleks perfect their first rudimentary time travel technology. They elect to use it to eliminate one of their perennial foes: Earth. Massing a force of 'expendable' guinea-pig Ogron mercenaries, a small group of Dalek volunteers travel back to Earth in the late 22nd century, shortly after the Dalek Invasion by the beta units was repelled. Aided by a paradox-built destabilization of Earth's government, they easily conquering the softened-up, recovering Earth.

These Daleks even boast to the Third Doctor about their acquisition of time travel, making it clear that this is their first subjective encounter with him while using it. They are, of course, thwarted, and their yolk lifted from the put-upon 22nd-century Earth. Back in the 'present,' the Daleks are unconcerned by this defeat; the jaunt back was a sufficient proof-of-concept. The secrets of time travel are now theirs, and they begin the construction of a limited number of taranium-powered timeships (very few in number due to the scarcity of the material).

However, they realize that their focus on humanity has been too narrow; so long as their enemy the Doctor remains at large, they will always know defeat. And so, they launch a campaign to use one to eliminate the other- one that will bring about their own downfall.

Traveling back from this point, well past 4000 AD, to the 1600s, they recruit professors Waterfield and Maxtible, and begin a tangled quest for the Human Factor... which eventually leads the Doctor return with them to Skaro in the 'present'- unknowingly, to the final days of their nearly two-millennia-old empire. There, the Doctor unleashes the destabilizing Human Factor on them, initiating a Dalek Civil War that is indeed their 'final end'- at least from the galaxy's perspective. From an objective viewpoint, in this original timeline, the Daleks cease to be a threat from this time forward, their menace ended at last.

But subjectively, many of the Doctor's other adventures are seeded from this catastrophic finale. Fleeing Daleks take to the few completed Dalek timeships, struggling to undo their dismal fate.

One group of Daleks, struggling against the infecting Human Factor (which accounts for their goofy behavior, as they fight to stave off their burgeoning, childlike humanity with the power of their racial superiority and hate) elect for the direct route. They chase the Doctor and his companions through time and space in a mad quest for vengeance- to destroy him before he can ever become the Second and bring about their downfall. This quest ends at Mechanus, where the infected Daleks are all eliminated, and their timeship destroyed.

Another group of survivors, uninfected and pure, manage the other timeship- and take a far more insidious route. Traveling back to the year 4000, this group of Daleks return to the height of the empire's power- bringing with them the pinnacle of Dalek temporal technology, the experimental Time Destructor. There (using alien allies due to their own small force, masquerading as emissaries from the contemporary Dalek Empire), they hatch a plan to alter history by conquering Earth. Bound by the inability to affect their own direct history (the Dalek Empire, unaware of their existence), nor to mine any taranium that will eventually be mined by the Daleks in the future and lead to the creation of their own time machine, they must rely on the small amount mined by Mavic Chen... which becomes the central object in an epic contest between the Doctor and his companions, starting on the planet Kembel and spanning all of time and space.

It is fitting that this attack represents the Daleks' last

true threat to the galaxy- their final, desperate, ultimate gambit using the pinnacle of their temporal technology. It makes both the epic scope of the tale, and the terrible sacrifices made in the final, apocalyptic, epic confrontation all the more meaningful.

This is not *quite* the end of the Daleks, however. As the planet Kembel succumbs to the ravages of unchecked temporal acceleration, a small contingent of Daleks left in the abandoned command center are able to shelter in the Dalek timeship, escaping- as the ship disintegrates around them, caught in the conflicting temporal field. It crashes, deep in the swamps of Vulcan, where it lays dormant for hundreds of years, the crew in near-death stasis (technology that Davros had already pioneered at the time he created them). These final survivors of the Dalek race are eventually found by the scientist Lesterson.

These Daleks have no master plan, no map for conquest... no ambitions save for starting again, gaining a foothold to rebuild their race. They fall back on static, an old technology harvested from the records of the failed beta Daleks- a technology that, it had been clearly demonstrated, could be created from the scraps of nothing. Despite this reliance on easily-built, ancient technology (not unlike the third Back to the Future film; making due with the materials of the era), these Daleks have knowledge of the most advanced of Dalek technologies, and parts harvested from the ruined timeship. Given time, they have the ability not only to start their race anew, but to restore its former heights of powers, even if they're currently stuck using the

Dalek equivalent of steampunk.

Until their plans hit one snag. The Doctor. And not only any Doctor, but the very one responsible for the downfall of Skaro! How their blood must have boiled!

But from the events of 'Evil of the Daleks,' they have learned well- adopting the simple manner that they observed from Human-Factored Daleks to allay suspicion, and taking well the lesson of a treacherous servant from Maxtible. They turn the very gambits that were the downfall of their Empire into tools in their service- and with guile, nearly succeed in the conquest of Vulcan.

In the end, however, the Doctor defeats them- and this seems, subjectively, to be their final televised story. However, these temporal experiments, like those of Space Station Chimera later will, have greatly disturbed the Time Lords, who see the potential for disaster. If even a single Dalek escapes- and they are notorious survivors- then their knowledge of time travel could lead to a catastrophic event.

Disturbed by the implications of Daleks with time travel, the Celestial Intervention Agency on Gallifrey embark on a campaign to curtail it, using their old patsy, the Doctor- whom they've become quite used to having as their errand boy. And just as the Daleks in 'Evil of the Daleks' were too clever for their own good, bringing about their own downfall with their oh-so-clever temporal gambit, the Time Lords fall into the same hubris trap.

And so, the Time War begins. No, not in the lost days of the McGann era... but in an act of pre-emptive warfare; an act of temporal espionage that indirectly serves as catalyst to all that follows.

As seen in 'Genesis of the Daleks,' the Fourth Doctor is sent back in time to alter Dalek history... which he does. From the Fourth Doctor era-onwards, the events that we've seen in other Dalek stories, all the ones that we've discussed so far, no longer exist.

Dalek history changes, irrevocably, creating an entirely new timeline in which the galaxy-conquerors of the original are absent. It also becomes surprisingly linear and easy to follow from this point, on to the end of the classic series. In this era, the adventures seem largely to occur in a chronological order for Doctor and Daleks alike. Once again, we return to the 1700s, during the war between the Thals and the Kaleds (a slight revision there; perhaps the oral history of the Thals mangled the name and remade it in their own image over the centuries). Mad scientist Davros enhances the rampant mutations present from the nuclear fallout on Skaro, forming and shaping it to create his 'master race' of Daleks. They turn on him, apparently exterminating him, as even he fails to meet their standards of racial purity.

However, intervention from the Doctor puts a bit of paranoia into Davros, and he takes precautions to survive this time, in a near-death suspended animation state-altering history. Meanwhile, the Daleks' history is further altered when they are sealed underground for a thousand years- a churning cauldron of hate, building, ready to erupt onto the galaxy a millennia-hence.

Worse for the Daleks, because of the Doctor's interference, they are unfinished. They still have the 'training wheels' on- mental conditioning and programming that Davros was using to indoctrinate them. Mental programming disseminated through the early PathWeb is now left switched on, constraining and shaping the will of the users within- robbing the Daleks of their conniving, hate-motivated intelligence.

They are no longer the canny betrayers of Kembel and Vulcan; instead, they are stuck with mental programming so rational and basic that it reduces their thought-processes to pedantic, logical circles. They think like machines- bereft of creativity, relying totally on the logic of their programming, so that even the Doctor mocks them as 'robots.' (Something that appeared for many years to be a baffling continuity error, with the author of the original Dalek stories forgetting their nature… until the missing piece of the puzzle fell into place with Asylum of the Daleks.)

This leaves them at a perpetual stalemate with the android Movellans (whom we can assume that the cannier Daleks originally steamrolled over in the first timeline; in fact, the android-duplicate creation abilities evidenced in 'The Chase' and 'Victory of the Daleks' may well have been learned from this conquest).

This protracted conflict checks the Dalek Empire's spread, leaving them less of a well-known, feared, galaxy-conquering menace than before. In fact, the Movellan War probably pre-empts a number of their empire-building stories; in this timeline, the 'beta' Daleks were never created. Earth was never invaded in the 22nd century. Mavic Chen probably lived a long life as a beloved, sane public figure. Lesterson may have innovated useful technology with his penchant for obsession directed somewhere more useful. And so forth- the history of Earth, un-harassed by the Daleks, was doubtless at its pinnacle in this timeline.

Eventually, the ongoing, stalemated conflict with the Movellans causes the Daleks, in desperation, to turn to the man that they betrayed- resurrecting Davros to be their creative spark. (This is, assuming our 1700s baseline, and another thousand years to dig out of the bunker, some time after the 26th century- perhaps around the 29th, allowing time for the Daleks to reach space, encounter the Movellans, and fight a long war. As the timetables continue, however, the actual years involved become less and less relevant... and less and less clear.)

Once again, the Doctor's meddling prevents the Daleks' plans from reaching fruition, and for another ninety years the war with the Movellans rages- culminating in an apparent Dalek defeat. Infected with a Dalek-specific virus, the Daleks (led by the Supreme Dalek) once again seek out the imprisoned Davros (some time around the 30th century), intending to use him to create a cure, and then destroy him.

Instead, Davros engineers another virus entirely- one which makes infected Daleks totally loyal to him. Armed with this splinter-cell of Davros-brainwashed Daleks, he escapes (presumably developing a cure in his exile).

The plot of the Time Lords has succeeded, to a degree. The Dalek Empire is a weak, fragmented thing- a pale shadow of its former glory. But the ultimate aim of the mission has failed- the Daleks have once again been driven by their defeats to develop time travel.

At this point, the war with the Movellans, one which has reduced the once-mighty Dalek Empire to a scattered group of roving bands before it could ever become the threat that it was in the original timeline... is dropped. It is not mentioned again. But with the advent of Dalek time corridor technology, it is not unreasonable to assume that the Daleks waged their first, successful Time War- eliminating the Movellan threat in the deep past in much the way that they were preemptively hobbled.

Now, though the conflict that defined the Dalek empire in the Second Timeline is over, the Daleks are not free from conflict. Davros' splinter cell of Daleks, skulking and experimenting in hiding, continue to fight a civil war against the Dalek Supreme-loyal, genetic-purity-minded Daleks back on Skaro. Two sets of Daleks warring against each other, one under the programming of Davros' rudimentary PathWeb, the other under the programming of his new virus. Two sets of Daleks without free will, battling against each other as Davros fights to remain on top.

Davros and his renegades are persecuted and harassed, with numerous assassins and Dalek agents making attempts on his life- to the point of creating a permanent decoy, apparently hobbled by the Movellan virus, to absorb any attacks on his life. He claims to have come straight from his escape with his Renegade Daleks to Necros- however, we can assume that either isn't true (Most likely a lie in order to protect other safehouses that Davros sheltered in, or the fact that he is using time travel).

Indeed, the Renegades have likely begun to conduct their fugitive flights via time corridors- and are from the future relative to the Imperial Daleks, as they recognize this incarnation of the Doctor in 'Revelation of the Daleks', while the Imperial Daleks do not. Davros clearly had to know about him in advance in order to set up a memorial-trap bearing his likeness. If the Doctor mockingly mentions that lame trap to Davros (not realizing it hasn't happened to Davros yet) at some point in his future and Davros' post-escape, pre-Necros past, it may have given Davros not only knowledge of this incarnation, but also of which face of the Doctor he'll next encounter on Necros, so that he can set up the trap. The joys of paradoxes...

Following this Necros encounter- where Davros loses a hand, a telling mark of continuity that lasts into the Time War and beyond- Davros is turned over to the Imperial faction... but apparently managed a turnaround. When we next see him, Davros leads the dominant 'Imperial' Daleks (the former Renegades, Davros-loyal Daleks that have retaken Skaro), while the 'Renegades' are now the traditional, purity-obsessed Daleks led by the Supreme Dalek- a hunted, harried band, just as Davros' forces had once been. The factions have changed positions.

As the Dalek Civil War intensifies, spilling out throughout time and space, both sides- stuck in another stalemate-begin to seek a trump card to end the conflict... history repeating itself.

This search leads them down a time corridor from the far-future of Skaro, the waning days of the Daleks (perhaps once again in the 39th+ century), to 1963 Earth, in the search for the Hand of Omega. This is not just an ultimate weapon; it is also key to expanding Dalek time travel abilities. The time corridors that they use, it seems, are clumsy and unstable ('crude and nasty,' as the Seventh Doctor notes)- not sufficient to prosecuting a true temporal war. *This* is the key to why they haven't yet used time travel to conquer the universe... but with the Hand of Omega, they could recreate Gallifreyan time travel abilities. The Daleks and their ambitions are clearly accelerating toward the Time War proper, with both unchecked time travel and an interest in Time Lord technology and its destructive potential at the forefront of their agenda.

Once again, the Davros-less Daleks, still hampered by their PathWeb programming, recruit a creative being to give them an advantage over their enemies. In this conflict, however, we see *both* factions dealt a severe blow; all of the Daleks are evidently destroyed, and Skaro itself is obliterated. This raises a host of issues- most specifically, the potential genocide of the Thal people, in their entirety.

We can only assume, with the total lack of concern or consideration on the Doctor's part for that once-integral people, that something has changed. Of course, we saw no appearance, nor mention of the Thals, in the follow-up to 'Genesis,' 'Destiny of the Daleks'- which was set on Skaro.

This lack of mention holds ominous portent.

In this new, second history, the Daleks were trapped underground in a bunker with a thousand years to stew and plan and plot, then burst forth on an unsuspecting world with no warning and all that bottled rage...

 We can assume that either the Thals were complacent and completely unprepared when the Daleks finally did break out- getting truly and wholly exterminated. The Doctor's intervention actually had a negative effect, giving the Thals a thousand years of peace, to become easy pickings for an unexpected Dalek invasion a millenia hence. The time period that Hartnell and the first TARDIS crew visited in 'The Daleks' is, quite likely, now only littered with Thal corpses.

Davros, meanwhile, escapes the end of 'Remembrance' to appear again later. More difficult is the apparent return of Skaro several times hence. In 'Asylum of the Daleks,' this is quite understandable- one might assume that one of the first changes wrought in the rampant temporal conflict of the Time War would be the Daleks' restoration of their homeworld.

However, we see Skaro alive and well in the TV Movie, 'pre-Time War,' as much as such a term can apply. This can only lead to the assumption that the Dalek Civil War from which both sides invaded in 'Remembrance' is somewhere in the far future of Dalek history- perhaps they are always fated to end up in a climactic civil war. Presumably, then, the brief opening scene of the TV Movie simply takes place at an earlier point in Skaro's history (before the 39th century)... but the planet remains fated for eventual destruction by the Hand of Omega in its future.

In many ways, the Time Lords' gambit had worked; a weaker Dalek empire, lacking creativity and bound by computer-logic, tied up first in a long war with the Movellans, and then by internal fighting, with Davros as a petty, selfish figure that weakened the Daleks by trying to twist them to his own ends. In the end, the empire was in shambles, its numerous wars of conquest erased from history in favor of constant battles for their own survival, and Skaro fated for eventual destruction... and all at the paltry cost of the Thal race. To the cold hearts of the Time Lord council, a bargain.

But the Daleks were soon to achieve their technological aims- after which the Time Lords would reap the whirlwind, a disaster of their own making.

The Daleks at last perfect their time travel- by means unknown, though based on the TV Movie, it may involve helium- and the Time War commences. Not the simple land war that we saw in its waning days, portrayed in The End Of Time and Day Of The Doctor.

No, the true Time War, almost impossible to portray on camera, would almost certainly be a war of temporal battlefields- going back in time to alter key events in cold-war-esque strikes (like the one seen in Genesis of the Daleks) as well as overt battlefields. The actual effects on the galaxy at large would almost certainly have been chaotic- like the continual revisions of 'Flesh and Stone' and 'Cold Blood,' on a much more immense scale. Reality constantly shifting and popping and changing as events in the past reshape it instantaneously. Time travel across the ages as Daleks try to avert the Time Lords' rise to power (more than likely trying to eliminate a young Omega and Rassilon, who would have been as certainly-protected as the creation time of the Daleks, and their emergence onto the surface of Skaro, would have been by the Dalek side). History re-written and re-re-written with every battle to control the past and reshape the present, until the fabric of time frayed an unleashed a host of paradoxes... and monstrosities, like the Nightmare Child, and the Could-Have-Been-King with his army of What-Ifs and Could-Have-Beens. Time coming apart at the seams as overlapping versions of reality sought to sort themselves out of the constant rewriting and temporal chaos.

Just as it was for the program of Doctor Who itself, the Time War serves as the great reset; restoring things that were lost and destroying things that were known. Intervention in the form of both Time Lord attacks and Dalek boosts reshapes Dalek history into an unknown new paradigm (pun intended). The Daleks appear to revise their own origins, returning to the crux point of 'Genesis' and eliminating their reliance on the PathWeb. They apparently restore themselves to an idealized version of their Empire, with the heights of their power from the First Timeline, and more. Racial purity becomes their rallying cry once again- yet oddly, there appears to remain a role for Davros in the

Time War. Though if the attitude of the Daleks in Journey's End is any indication, it is a marginalized one.

Regardless, a Third Timeline is clearly forged; one of the Daleks' own making, tempered by whatever restraint the Time Lords' efforts can put on it. Skaro is restored. The Dalek Empire exists once again, rampaging throughout time with the height of its temporal technology. The Daleks rise, and conquer... and eventually, fall, en masse, in all-out immolation as Gallifrey falls with them.

All save for a single Dalek soldier... and the Emperor's burning flagship. The two may even have been one and the same- a single Dalek falling away from the damaged craft as it fell back through time; crashing to Earth in the 20th century. The saucer may even have arrived around the same time, beginning its centuries-long wait in the dark.

Just as we don't know for sure which of the 60s and 70s First Timeline Dalek stories still happened in the Second Timeline (some almost certainly didn't, but others did), we don't know how many of the Second Timeline 80s Dalek stories still ocurred in the post-Time-War Third... and how much of it was contianed within the Time Lock, never to touch the universe beyond.

Thus, we can suppose that the Third Timeline, beginning with Christopher Eccleston's era, may not contain anything that came before it; a very different, and very mysterious history of the Empire that is nearly impossible to recount due to its constant self-revisions.

And even this Third Timeline has a bit of a false start- an

adventure with Van Statten in 2012 that may or may not come to pass.

This timeline in itself is fraught with chaos- the 2012 events of 'Dalek' appear to have been wiped out by the ousting of Harriet Jones, leaving only the events of 'Parting of the Way'-onwards through 'Journey's End' in the actual timeline. (In short, everything bad that ever happened to the Tenth Doctor was, potentially, brought down on his head by that act of hubris and those six golden-age-stealing words. Without Harriest Jones to keep a tight leash on Torchwood, Daleks were released, and Rose was lost; with the position vacant, and Martha traveling instead of Rose, the Master had an opening to return and take power. The former (Daleks) led to Journey's End, and the loss of Donna, and the latter to End of Time, and the regeneration.) Either way, it seems that Van Statten- and the world- didn't know about the existence of Daleks yet because the Doctor was in a timeline where they were never unleashed in 2008... because he hadn't done so yet. After 'Doomsday,' history is changed. The 2012 that he visited no longer existed, overwritten by the new one resulting from his actions in 'Army of Ghosts' and 'Doomsday.' Once again, the Marty McFly experience.

So, due to this chain of causality, the Cult of Skaro is released from the void- fighting a failed battle with the Cybermen that devestates Cannary Wharf. With the Dalek forces pulled from the void and then sucked back into it, the Cult flees to 1920s Earth (much as their First Timeline predecessors once fled the Human Factor disaster to

Kembel and Vulcan, to rebuild from scratch). Following their near-extinction, the lone survivors restored Davros from the Time War, some time in the past.

During the 21st century of Earth, then, there are two Dalek forces in exitence- Davros' Daleks, built from cells of his own body, and the Emperor's Daleks, built from cells of failed gameshow contestants. Two groups of Time War survivors, each with a faction of scratch-built Daleks, waiting in the deep void and building their strength.

This ongoing 'scavenger' period features the repeated rise of grand Dalek armies, followed by the immediate 'total extinction of the species,' in a rather melodramatic series of reversals... until finally, one of the factions is ready to bide its time no longer. Davros' Daleks steal a numbe rof planets in the plan to enact his new weapon- a reality bomb that eliminate all life in the galaxy, save for his followers. In 2008, the Daleks invade Earth once more- for the first time, in this Timeline.

And all the while, the mad Emperor and his worshipers wait in the dark, biding their time and continuing to prepare. There, in the void, they wait almost another 199,000 years... ironically, in their madness and genetic impurity, far removed from anything Dalek and utterly devoid of conquest, they manage to outlast any Dalek Empire that came before, only revealing themselves in the 2,000th century- a mind-boggling 1,998 millenia longer-lived than the mighty empires of old. But, thanks to the Bad Wolf, they are soon dust... and it seems that, like the First Timeline, the Daleks have been fully destroyed in the distant future.

But the Daleks have already become an intergal part of future history through individuals like Adelaide Brooke-making their subsequent erasure through the Cracks in the universe somewhat problematic. As the mechanism of this erasure is somewhat unclear, we can only speculate-ironically, the erasure of the Dalek invasion may render 'Dalek,' with Daleks unknown in 2012, back into the timeline... and ought to result in a restored, unendangered Donna Noble, and a Rose Tyler still searching the universe for her love (with that Metacrisis nonsense undone).

The vaugaries of this process, and the reboot of the the Big Bang 2.0 in 'The Big Bang'- unexplored and unlikely to ever be- leave us with very little real idea of the final result. It may have, potentially, permanently excluded things like Cyberkings and Dalek invasions (one wonders if Rose would still be on Earth and Adelade will never be going to Bowie Base One if those events are removed from history, though); though those events might have been restored in the Big Bang (causing one to wonder why the history books don't record the rampage of the Cyberking).

So it is ambiguously and uncertainly that we posit the possible genesisof a Fourth Dalek Timeline (which may actually be a continuation of the Third, if all crack-erased events were restored). If there is a Fourth, it begins with 'Victory of the Daleks.' With the events of 'Doomsday' and 'Journey's End' apparently having been erased, it's likely that these were 'atheist' breakaways from the mad Emperor during his millenia-long wait (as this is the only source of Time War survivors without the events of Doomsday).

On the other hand, if the events of those two episodes *were* restored by the Big Bang and this is merely a continuation of the Third Timeline, then the Daleks posing as Ironsides may also have been survivors of the DoctorDonna's magical genocide control panel (which would fit with that Timeline's penchant for exagerated 'every single one of them died' claims that turned out not to be true.)

It's even possible that some of the many Daleks invading Gallifrey (as seen in 'Day of the Doctor') when it was pulled out of the time lock in 'End of Time' managed to slip away and reach safety when Gallifrey was pulled back into the time lock.

Whatever their origin, they locate the progenitor devices (either created by Davros and seeded during his long-void wait developing the reality bomb, or slipping past the time lock as a backup plan in case of Dalek loss during the Time War).

This results in the brightly-colored 'new paradigm' Daleks, who, with their unmonitored, unrestricted use of Time Travel, were able to instantly propagate themselves throughout history, resulting in a Dalek Empire as strong and deadly as before. Though 'Victory' is ambiguous in its timeline, the results of the escape at the end well and truly inaugurate a Fourth, shaped by the Daleks with crude and imprecise time corridor technology- which doesn't allow them to conquer the unvierse, but does allow them to establish themselves at a very early point.

This Fourth Timeline, based on references in 'Asylum of the Daleks,' seems to have formed in a very simillar manner to the First Timeline, with a number of those old 60s and 70s adventures being restored to the time-stream... bringing the Daleks full-circle, as it were.

In this new post-paradigm, time-skewed version of the Empire, the Daleks have a parliament- a form of governance that they never had before. We can assume that this change from the traditional Imperial and Supreme power-base is a new concept introduced by the 'new paradigm' Daleks... who, ironically, to all appearences, have fallen out of favor with that government, giving rise to the bronze units once more. Is a racial-purity Civil War once more around the corner for the Daleks?

'Asylum of the Daleks' encapsualtes the hybrid nature of this fourth timeline nicely, showcasing survivors from Kembel, Spiridon, Vulcan, and others- affirming that at least some of the adventures from the classic series still occurred in this timeline... but also showing them as modern bronze Daleks, attesting to apparent revisionist history through the case of the Time War. (Unless they were just given new, refurbished cells to be imprisoned in, for some reason). We may assume that the events of the First Timeline continued unchecked, even up to and including the Human Factor disaster and the 'Final End'- after which the new paradigm Daleks rebuilt the Empire from scratch, estchewing the abandoned Skaro, bearing signs of the 39th century alpha-

Dalek Empire for a mobile, saucer-based civilization.

'Asylum' also demonstrates the Dalek conversion processes. This curious process mirrors techniques used by Davros in 'Revelation of the Daleks' and the Dalek Emperor in 'Parting of the Ways'... but stands utterly counter to the purity-standards of the new paradigm. This is a process that we've only seen used by madmen who do not hold to true Dalek standards. To see it used here- unless we are meant to assume that the insane inhabittants of the asylum developed and applied the technique to Clara on their own and that it is not standard Dalek practice- may hint at a shift in Dalek culture... and the reason that the new paradigm units have fallen out of favor. It could hint that a new Civil War is indeed just around the corner; a ying-yang counterpart to the discovery of time travel which always seems to arrive in the latter days of the Dalek Empire. This may not be a pattern that they're capable of breaking.

The Doctor is given a clean slate as the Dalek knowledge of him- from all timelines- is erased, giving him a fresh start... which is apparently subsequently undone during the protracted Seige of Trenzalor, with the records of the Papal Mainframe replenishing their familliarity.

The scope of the setback dealt to them in that story is uncertain; was the destroyed mega-saucer the same one seen in 'Asylum,' housing the Parliament and Prime Minister? Have the Daleks been decimated, or merely suffered the annoying-but-harmless loss of a single ship? Only time will tell- as will the nature of this setback to the Doctor's plans to 'step back into the shadows,' and the relationship that they and Capaldi will enjoy. Technically, the Emperor is still out there, waiting with his mad disciples- still existant in this history, cloistered away. And the Dalek Empire. whatever blow it was dealt, seems to be thriving anew under the new paradigm, as the Dalek Empire hasn't since the 30th century of the First Timeline.

One thing is clear: the Daleks will almost certainly have to be change again if the Time Lords are returning, lest the Time War simply re-ignite; whatever is going to happen, yet another 'New paradigm' seems almost inevitably in store. Perhaps a Fifth Timeline, stripping the Daleks of their temporal technology and resetting all this history once more awaits us.

And that, in a very-long nutshell, is Dalek history. At least thrice-revised, filled with uncertain changes and hand-waved blanks... but progressing in an *almost*-comprehensible manner. With the exception of a few estbalished chronological sequences (such as the classic series' Davros stories), many Dalek stories can be placed in any order, to the user's taste. This accounting is, by no means, a definitive recounting of Dalek history chronilogically... merely the most logical order in which it can be reconstructed, from the point of view of this author. Many others could come up with many other orders- each as supported and unsupported by the vaugaries of Dalek history as the next.

Reagrdless, this newest timeline if filled with potential- a brand new Doctor, yet to encounter his most infamous foe for the first time, and a Dalek paradigm that allows the story to go in almost any direction; an open-ended status quo and a fresh canvas.

As for the Doctor- whatever elements of Dalek history have been erased, whichever ones still survive- whether Dalek Invasion of Earth will still happen in 2064 in this timeline, or the Time War still happened the same way or not after eh 'changed his mind'- one thing is for certain. Every variation, every event in each of the four... the Doctor remembers them all. As far as he's concerned, every one of them happened. And for every one of them that the universe as a whole *didn't* experience in this timeline- for every event that they were *spared*- he is almost certainly grateful.

7 THE COOKBOOK OF RASSILON

by Taylor Elliott

Grace's San Francisco Sourdough Scones

2 1/2 cups bread flour
1/2 teaspoon salt
1 teaspoon cream of tartar
1 teaspoon baking soda
1/4 cup white sugar
1/3 cup cold butter, cut into very small pieces
2 tablespoons milk
6 oz grated gruyere cheese
1/4 cup dried blueberries
1/4 cup chopped pecans
1 1/2 cups sourdough starter

Preheat oven to 400F (200C). Line a baking sheet with parchment paper.

Whisk together the flour, salt, cream of tartar, baking soda, sugar.

Cut in the butter with the side of a spatula, a knife, or a pastry blender until the mixture resembles coarse crumbs. Add the sourdough starter and mix by hand to form a soft dough. Mix in the gruyere, blueberries, and pecans.

Turn the dough out onto a lightly floured surface and divide it into 4 even pieces. Pat or roll one piece of dough into a 1/2-inch thick round -- use a cake pan as a guide if you need to! You only have one life. No need to waste it on silly things like trying to hand shape scones.

Cut the round into 4 wedge-shaped pieces and place the scones on the prepared baking sheet about 1 inch apart. Repeat with remaining pieces of dough. Brush the tops of the scones with milk and sprinkle with additional cheese, if desired.

Bake 12 to 15 minutes, or until scones just begin to turn golden brown.

Regeneration Potion

1 part Prosecco (or other sparkling wine of your choice)
2 parts Midori
1 part Bicardi 151
1 part Averna (or other Amaro)
2 tbsp Lime juice Ground ginger Sugar

Mix the ginger and sugar together in a shallow dish, and use some of your lime juice to rim the glass with it. In a cocktail shaker, combine the remaining lime juice, rum, Midori, and Amaro. Pour into glass. Top off with Prosecco, and become the soldier you need to be.

"No More"

1 part Grenadine
1 part Campari
1 part Goldschlager

Layer the grenadine, Campari, and Goldschlager into a shot glass. Admire your shiny red button, and declare no more (to sobriety).

Rose's Favorite Chips and Slitheen Sauce

Chips

5 medium potatoes
1 liter of cooking oil

Cut your potatoes into healthy sized chips. Place the chips in a colander and rinse under cold running water.

Place the chips in a pan of cold water, and bring to a gentle boil, simmering for 3-4 minutes. Drain with a colander and pat dry.

Heat the oil to 250 F (120 C) in a deep fryer or other suitable vessel. Remember: safety first! Use oils appropriate to frying, and use a large, heavy-bottomed pan!

Blanch the chips in small batches for a few minutes -- do not brown them. After approximately two minutes per batch, place the chips on a draining rig.

When ready to serve, heat your oil to 400 F (200 C) and fry for 5-8 minutes until golden brown. Enjoy with your tightwad alien boyfriend.

Slitheen Sauce

1 teaspoons anchovy paste
1 small garlic clove, minced
1/2 cup sour cream
1/2 cup mayonnaise
1/4 cup heavy cream
1/2 cup parsley
1/8 cup tarragon
1/8 cup basil
4 tbsp chives
2 tsp ground mustard
1 tsp ground ginger
2 tbsp lemon juice
2 tbsp lime juice Salt and pepper to taste

Place all ingredients in a blender or food processor and blend until smooth and creamy. Know that, if alarmed, your sauce may produce a poison dart -- just be prepared to dodge it.

Reinette's Rissoles and Apple Relish

Rissoles

1 1/2 cups ground chicken
1 leek
1 tablespoon fresh sage, finely chopped
1/3 cup breadcrumbs

Instruct your kitchen servants to finely chop the leek and combine it with the chicken, chopped sage, breadcrumbs, salt, and pepper in a large bowl. Using your (their, obviously -- king's consorts do not dally with such nonsense!) hands, shape them into small rissoles. Set aside.

Heat a large skillet, lubricated with oil, over medium-high heat and cook the rissoles for 3-5 per side, or until cooked through.

Apple Relish

2 apples, chopped into small pieces
3 tbsp brown sugar
1 tsp lemon juice
1 tbsp apple cider vinegar
1 tsp ground cumin

Combine all ingredients into a saucepan over medium-high heat, stirring until sugar has dissolved. Reduce heat to low and simmer until apples are tender.

Serve your rissoles alongside your apple relish and enjoy with your fellow courtiers while waiting for your lonely angel to return to you.

Martha's Revenge

1 pear, cored and sliced thin
1/2 cup butter, melted
2 tbsp cinnamon
1 cup brown sugar

4 egg yolks
4 egg whites, beaten to stiff peaks
2 1/4 cups warm milk
1/2 cup cake flour
1/2 cup confectioner's sugar
1 stick butter, melted and cooled
1 tbsp vanilla

Grease a cake pan and preheat your oven to 350 F.

Mix 1/2 cup melted butter, brown sugar, and cinnamon. Arrange pears in a thin, even layer on the bottom of the pan, then pour sugar mixture over them, careful not to disturb your pattern.

Mix the egg yolks, powdered sugar, and vanilla until the mixture becomes very pale and thick. Add lemon zest, then the remaining melted butter, mixing until the mixture begins to thicken again. Gradually add the warm milk, a third at a time, until well incorporated. Sift in the flour and mix over medium speed until just incorporated. Do not over mix.

In another bowl with a clean set of beaters, whip egg whites to stiff peaks. Carefully fold into the remaining batter. Pour gently over the pears and sugar. Bake for ten minutes at 350, then lower heat to 325 and bake for another 50 minutes, or until a toothpick comes out clean from the center.

Cool completely and allow to rest in the refrigerator overnight before serving to ungrateful Time Lords who strand you as a chambermaid while they make gooey eyes at some school marm.

Sparkling Cyanide

2 parts Seltzer Water
1 part Orgeat syrup
1 part Light rum (optional) Sprig of mint

Combine and serve in a tall glass over ice, garnishing with mint. Prepare to stimulate your enzymes into reversal.

Crack-in-Time TARDIS Brittle

1 cup white sugar
1/2 cup light corn syrup
1/4 tsp salt
1/4 cup water
1 cup dried blueberries
2 tbsp butter, softened
1 tsp baking soda
Blue food dye

Grease large cookie sheet and line with parchment paper.

In a heavy saucepan, over medium heat, bring sugar, corn syrup, salt, and water to a boil. Stir in blueberries and food dye. Place candy thermometer on the side of the pot.

Stir frequently until mixture reaches 300 F (150 C). Remove from heat, and immediately stir in baking soda and butter. Pour onto cookie sheet. Using forks, carefully pull into an even, rectangular shape, and allow to cool. Smash into smaller pieces. Prepare for silence to fall.

Fish Fingers and Custard

1 package ladyfingers
2 cups graham crackers, crushed fine
2 cups milk
2 egg yolks
1 whole egg
1/4 cup sugar
1/4 cup cornstarch
1/3 cup sugar
2 tbsp butter
1/2 cup heavy cream
1 pinch salt
1 tsp vanilla 1 tsp nutmeg

In a heavy saucepan, dissolve 1/4 cup sugar into milk. Bring to a boil.

In a medium bowl, whisk together the egg yolks and egg, then stir in the sugar and cornstarch until the mixture is smooth.

When the milk has come to a boil, cut the heat on the stove and carefully drizzle the hot milk into the eggs while mixing. Be careful not to cook the eggs!

Place the whole mixture into the saucepan and slowly bring to a boil, stirring constantly so that it does not curdle or scorch.

Once mixture has boiled and thickened, remove

from heat and stir in butter, vanilla, and nutmeg. Divide approximately in half. Cover one half with plastic and place in the refrigerator. With the other half, whisk in heavy cream until mixture is smooth.

Place ladyfingers in single layer in a shallow dish and pour the custard cream mixture over them. Place in the refrigerator and allow to chill for at least three hours. This is an excellent time to go check on that crack in your wall.

When ready to serve, preheat oven to 350 and grease a baking sheet. Remove ladyfingers from custard mixture (they should be soft but still firm enough to handle) and roll in crushed graham crackers. Bake for 10-15 minutes, or until "fish fingers" are warm and the outside is crunchy. Serve alongside custard to the strange man who fell out of a box that fell from the sky.

River's "Sweetie" Pie

Unbaked pie crust 3 eggs 1/2 cup butter, softened 1 1/2 cups white sugar 3 tbsp all-purpose flour 1 cup buttermilk 1 tsp vanilla 1 tbsp lemon juice 1/4 tbsp nutmeg 1 tbsp ground ginger 3/4 tbsp ground cayenne

Preheat oven to 350 F (175 C).

Beat eggs until frothy, then add butter and sugar. Slowly incorporate flour and beat until smooth.

Stir in buttermilk, vanilla, lemon juice, and spices. Pour into your pie shell.

Bake for 50 minutes, or until center is firm. Enjoy watching your guests when they realize their dessert has a hell-in-high-heels kick.

Clara's Souffle

1/2 cup cake flour
1/2 cup unsweetened dark cocoa
1/2 tsp baking powder
5 ounces semisweet chocolate chips
2 sticks butter, cut into small pieces
3 large eggs
1 egg white
1 tsp vanilla
3/4 cup sugar
1/3 tsp salt
4 tbsp Nutella

Preheat the oven to 350 F (140 C) and grease four 7 ounce ramekins. Prepare a roasting pan that these ramekins fit comfortably in, and begin heating a kettle or pot of water.

In a small bowl, whisk the flour, cocoa, and baking powder together.

In a microwave safe bowl or on the stove, cook the chocolate chips and butter, stirring frequently, until smooth.

Beat the eggs, egg white, vanilla, sugar, and salt until mixture becomes pale yellow and fluffy -- about five minutes. Slowly incorporate chocolate mixture, then the flour mixture, until everything is well incorporate and smooth.

Spoon enough batter to fill each ramekin halfway, drop a tablespoon of Nutella into the center of each, and take a moment to ignore the Daleks (or nagging children) at your door. Spoon remaining batter evenly amongst ramekins.

Place the ramekins in the roasting pan, and fill with approximately 1/2" of the hot water.

Bake for 30 minutes, until the soufflés have risen and are slightly cracked on top. Share with your mother or favorite Time Lord, or eat them all yourself and tell anyone who asks that they were too beautiful to live.

8 NEVER GO ON WALKS

Johnathan Viceroy was going on one of those walks whose main point was to get out of the house and pretend he might run into someone he knew, while in reality he was very aware he wasn't going to run into anyone, especially because he was in the park at this time of night. It was perhaps unfortunate then that he did run into someone, as the hole in reality tore open, spewing blue energy through the air and along the ground, causing some terrified squirrels to scamper away into the cold night from their cozy nooks in the trees. Vice naturally stared, as holes in the fabric of time and space were not particularly common where he lived, and he had in fact not only never seen one before, but had no idea what it was. He stepped towards it, the energy pulsing and swirling like a whirlpool, and then thought better of stepping towards it any further, which turned out to be an incredibly good move.

In one swift second- a large chunk of metal and cloth shot out of the tear, and landed twenty feet away, where it bounced once and skidded to a halt near the band shell where the free summer orchestra concerts were held, and the tear sealed up with a sort of zipping slurping sound that was unfortunately not the kind of noise one would take seriously at all, with a small pop at the end like a comic gag. This left Vice staring at the thing that had just shot out of the tear, which began to slowly push itself up until it collapsed again, as the coat it had been wearing lazily rolled around in the grass with the light wind.

Vice ran over to the prone ball of metal which was starting to look less like a ball than a person. His first inclination was to say the person was some sort of cosplayer, but as Vice reminded himself, cosplayers don't generally drop out of glowing blue holes in reality.

As he moved closer, he could hear a very faint whirring sound, like the fan on a laptop. The figure was coated entirely in some sort of dark plating the color of a turned off television set. It was only when the figure's skin started to blaze with light and error ridden images in brief bursting flickers that vice realized the plating was made of TV screens... Or something like them. From head to toe it was coated, with some of the plates being larger, like on the chest, and some being very fine, like the layers of interlocking or overlayed screens on the joints. It could be a man in a suit, there were no odd places where a body part would be clearly missing, but the armor seemed even from a distance like an extension of the being's body rather than an outer layer. Where there would have been a face was an oval mask made of the same material with one electronic eye on the left side of the face (or maybe "camera" was the correct term, electric eye always sounded so 1960's). The figure was huge as well, maybe six foot five inches, though not particularly broad shouldered or skinny, so from a distance you might not notice. It was also very muscular, if what was under that plating was muscle. The figure gave a slight twitch, which give Vice a start, and he was startled again when he heard a low moan from behind him.

Turning quickly, and with a divine lack of grace, he saw a young woman framed in the dual light of the moon and the slowly shrinking blue hole, her hand on her obviously throbbing head as she got up, wobbling from side to side on shaky legs. She was wearing a grey skirt-suit with a black tie, and her black hair was heavily disheveled, hanging loosely over features Vice had an instant inclination to call Slavic.

"Are you okay miss?"

She didn't respond, and just blinked, tilting her head around as though getting used to the light, or her new surroundings, or just trying to get a focus on anything, though truthfully all three of those things.

"Miss?" He edged closer to her.

She looked towards him then past him, and sloppy ran towards the figure on the ground, awkwardly shoving Vice to the side as he reached toward her. She knelt at the figure, equal parts nurse and technician, and pulled up some sort of menu on the screen on the being's chest. Vice had been hoping she would start narrating her actions, or explaining what on earth she was doing, as through there was an audience she was catering to, but no such luck. She just cursed a few times, pulled out a Phillips head screwdriver, and tried pulling open a panel and fiddling with something, which apparently didn't do anything.

"Do you need any help?" He added, limply.

She finally looked towards him, her chest heaving heavily as she gritted her teeth. "Where are we?"

"Um, the park?" Vice said, hoping that was helpful, then added, "Feldling park?"

"What nation? What planet? What year?"

Vice was actually starting to get into the groove of this, after all he'd seen plenty of science fiction before, and while what was going on was certainly outside of his realm of knowledge, it certainly seemed to fit the genre.

"Er, United States of America. Deer Ridge Illinois, if that matters. Earth. November 22nd, 2013."

She simply nodded, and stared off into the grass where the coat was still lightly bouncing in an almost jovial way, it and the wind seemed to be the only things there having a decidedly good time.

"I need you to take me somewhere we can rest. Not a hospital."

"Are you sure you don't need a hospital?" He said, noting to him self there was a bit of blood on her lip and scalp. In response, she pulled out a gadget from her purse, and flicked a switch on it. From it burst a hologram of a cat, and not one of those stringy holograms you see on television, it looked like a real tiny cat just sitting there rotating above her palm.

"Does this look like something you'd see at the store? We're not from around here if you haven't noticed." Vice nodded. "I'll um, call my girlfriend."

* * * *

Miranda Rodriguez was asleep when Vice called her, and hadn't been happy to go out to a park she didn't like in the middle of the night. Her fears that he might try doing something stupid like try to propose to her after waking her up from a perfectly good dream about going to a pancake house that was also her High School were luckily dashed when it turned out he had simply found a cyborg and an office worker who were presumably from the future while walking around in the park. By the time she got there in her car, the Cyborg was online again, and running through some sort of color test on its skin plates. Vice waved at her, and she just stared back at.

"What on Earth?"

"Miranda, thank God. Meet Graelyn Scythes, and Archimedes..." he paused, and the hulking figure finished his sentence for him, "Artemis VonAhnerabe." Miranda just nodded slowly, "I know, its quite the mouthful."

"We really do need to get out of here though...." Graelyn said, through the dried blood on her lip.

"Er, we do? Is that hole thing like... Spilling radiation or something?"

Graelyn shook her head, "No, we're being followed. Can you get up Arch?" Arch stood up, with a slight whir. Vice turned to Miranda, "Can we take them to your place? My apartment isn't really that big." She nodded, "Yeah, of course..." As Arch and Graelyn started following them towards Miranda's car, the hole in the universe (which had been shrinking) began expanding. "Run." Graelyn said, her eyes widening, reflecting back the blue light and the moonlight. Miranda began to say something, when something else shot out of the hole, rolling through the grass and bouncing off the rock in a way that would have reminded her of a ball if it wasn't for the metal clang it made as it did so. Finally the form hit the ground in a jumble of limbs. Whatever it was, it looked like Archimedes, only the plates on that figure were colored a deep black at the moment, a black that made the night sky look downright colorful. "Should we help it?"

"No." Graelyn spat out. "Run. Like hell."

Whatever the anti-Arch was, it was getting up. Its plates slid into their proper place on its body, its shoulder popping back into place from where it had slid out upon impact. From each of its forearms a blade slid out above the wrist. It advanced.

They didn't need to be told twice-- Vice and Miranda ran like hell towards the car, with Graelyn close behind, cursing as her office shoes proved exactly how much they weren't meant for running. Miranda whipped her keys out, and they slid out of her hand and dashed on the door window. She scampered to pick them up as Vice slid into the passenger seat she opened the door and slid them into the ignition, failing to line it up right the first time. Vice looked over at her, his eyes were huge. Graelyn seemed to struggle with how to open the door for a moment before getting in herself, yelling "Arch! ARCH!" through the still open door. In their panic, neither Vice nor Miranda had noticed Archimedes heading towards his opposite, and now the pair of them were facing off against each other like two gunslingers in the old west, only with swords, so maybe that wasn't the best analogy. Arch had extended identical blades from his own arms, his coat billowing gently in the breeze in a way that seemed almost too intentional to be co-incidence.

Vice looked between Graelyn and Archimedes, and

though the metal man had no facial expression, he could tell Graelyn knew exactly what Arch meant as he turned his head to meet her gaze and gave a curt nod. If Graelyn had been some other person, she might have shown sorrow on her face. Instead she just looked more empty as she yelled the word, "Drive," not taking her eyes off of Archimedes.

The two metal men started walking, then running, then they leaped at each other, their clash in the air making a sound that was far clearer than their forms as the car zoomed out away from the park, past the hospital, through neighborhoods, until all sight and sound had vanished.

It was only then that he could hear Graelyn make a small 'hic' sound, like she was holding something back. But when he turned to look, she may has well have been a stone statue to compliment the metal ones.

Part 2: Homemaking, 2000 and Some AD

She staggered through the door, and collapsed onto Miranda's couch, loosening the buttons on her clothes, and throwing off her shoes. Her stockings, which were only even vaguely recognizable as stockings because in the light of the apartment you could make out all of the holes in them. Whatever they were made of, it looked just like her skin was peeling off like a snake.

"Okay, I need to know what is going on." Miranda said, louder than she'd intended, "-And not just the cliff notes version."

Graelyn groaned, "Could I at least had some tea? Or some vodka?" Vice just went off to the kitchen to start heating it

up, someone had to do it. As he shuffled through the
cupboards, he could hear most of what followed:
"You're really not going to believe me."
"Try me.
Earl Grey? Would she like Earl Grey? Everyone liked Earl
Grey... Except for one unpleasant Ex-Girlfriend he had.
Better not chance it, Earl Grey seemed a good judge of
character.
"I'm from a future."
"Like the year 3000?"
"A future, not The future, which would imply your future.
And not as far as the year 3000, no."
He couldn't see her, but Vice knew Miranda had crossed her
arms, "A future? What kind of ridiculousness is that?"
"Alternate universes. Parallel realities. Do you not have
science fiction in this universe?"
"We have science fiction."
"That's what that hole was, a tear in realities."
The kettle was nearly boiling. Vice picked out a mug: there
were not many options, a pink mug with doughy eyed
kitties, a mug with the mascot of a college neither he nor
Miranda was a fan of, and a mug depicting Shakespeare
dressed as a hip hop artist. Sadly, the Kitten mug was
probably the most tasteful.
"So you're telling me you and that robot-"
"-He's not a robot!" Graelyn sounded passionate for half a
moment before slipping back into her cool demeanor, "He's
a cyborg. A human augmented with technology in order to
facilitate superior performance in tasks."
"And what sort of tasks was he built for? Those weren't

pruning sheers."

"Of course not. He's a weapon, one I happened to luck out on finding."

"A weapon?"

"Well he's not a soldier."

"And who is following him?"

Teabags in the water... Would she like sugar? Usually he'd ask. Somehow that didn't seem appropriate. Milk did though. He grabbed the jug out of the fridge and poured a splash in, watching the white turn a gentle brown.

"Ares. He's another one of the experiments..."

Hundreds of Years Later...

Archimedes ran across the rooftops of the city, leaping between the gaps of alleys and streets. His heavy metal feet leaving gentle cracks in some of the older buildings, and occasionally even footprints like he was an astronaut bounding across the moon. Turning his head to look behind him, he may as well have been on the moon as Ares leapt across the last gap with an ease that would have made Olympians cry. Ares' landed perfectly, never taking his eyes off of Archimedes, and barreled towards him. Arch looked back just in time to shift the pistons in his legs into gear and catapult himself onto the next roof. The wind rushed past at a weird angle, as the lights of holographic advertisements reflected off his skin.

The wind was no anomaly, at an odd angle to his left the above ground metro line was running, levitating just slightly above its magnetic rails. Running for it would mean going at an angle that would let Ares close distance... But

Archimedes couldn't keep this run up forever. The train had long ago vanished, long ago for a train that went hundreds of miles an hour, but there would be another one in just a moment, he could see it off in the distance and the range finding software in his skull calculated the timing of the jump perfectly. He ran, his body moving at exactly the right pace, the motors elegantly adjusting for the minutest changes in the environment.

He jumped.

If you were watching right then, your eyes on the scene, you wouldn't have seen the train at all. Lets say you were hunkered away, tapped into the city's security camera system-- no, better yet into that and the electronic eyes of the two men involved in the chase, all you would have seen was a metal man leaping into the open air, with no where to land but a thin metal pole surging with electricity that wound its way far into the distance of the city, and then a sudden quick blur and a noise, and from the security cameras you would have seen nothing then, as though the man had just disappeared. Luckily, you had his eye as well, and that was pointed at the side of a train car, where a baffled couple who both had spiked hair stared in complete and utter bafflement at the camera, which shook slightly from the speed. You wouldn't be worried about the man-- no, the experiment, to you-- attached to the camera, as you knew the robotic hands were not only strong enough to hold on, but could magnetize themselves at will.

"Its not going as well as I thought it might." You might say, swirling the glass of wine you were holding. The man nearby, the one from Central America with the slick hair, would give a non-committal shrug, "This one, what is his name?"

"Archimedes," said a bored looking woman with more money than anyone else in the room. She continued scrolling through the book she was reading on her tablet. "Yes, yes. Archimedes. He is, how would you say... an outlier. We're getting rid of him with this little trial."

"An outlier how?" You would ask tersely.

"Well, you know that he and the others have been raised in a space station, you know, to make them think that the Earth is gone and they are the only survivors, my idea, one which might bear further consideration for-"

"We all know about your future plans," the woman added, "just get on with it."

"Right, well, we removed all of the experiments from the space station in order to finish their training for combat and infiltration missions here on Earth where we could, you know, monitor them better. Bring in our best." He would slip an arm around your shoulder, as though you were best pals (though you would have only met that day), and give you his best smile. You'd return it, obviously, forcing your teeth out all the way. You would still not quite understand these humans and their needless touching.

"I take it then, that you screwed up and this Archimedes got left behind?"

"It was a fortuitous accident though, see-"

"We left his whole family there and had to conduct an op to kill them all." The man would scowl at the woman before putting his smile back on.

"And the op missed him to?"

"Er, no, he killed them all. But now that is all finished, and its enabled us to run a test of him against one of our fully primed models. We just had to lure him back to Earth with secrets of his past, or whatnot."

You would look skeptically back at the video screens, where it was apparent Ares had managed to hitch a ride on the train as well, and was scooting along the side of it slowly towards Archimedes, who was trying desperately to figure out a way to get out of this situation. The primitives would assume you'd be interested in this at all, seeing this in their three-dimensional way, and you'd feign interest to keep them properly in the dark.

Ares reached Archimedes, and his arm stretched out, a blade shooting out of it, and Arch just let go. He fell carefully, followed by Ares, and smashed through a window of an office building, where a woman holding a hologram dropped it, her mouth open in shock, the glowing light model of a face not even hitting the ground before Ares came in through the same hole, and Archimedes bulldozed a desk and leapt out a different window, catching hold of a passing air-car, followed by Ares, who barely gripped the edge of it. The two of them began fighting, swords shooting out of their arms to clash violently, climbing on top of the car, their magnetic feet holding on perfectly. The driver inside screamed, and ejected, sending the car spinning. Something happened, it was unclear exactly what, maybe a foot got put in the wrong place now that there was a hole in the roof leading to the car's controls, but it zoomed off, its speed becoming not only illegal but probably deadly, and as the sword fight drug on, it became apparent there was no land.

Then Ares struck the roof under Arch's feet.

It was a simple move, and a dangerous one, as a chunk of the car ripped off and fell far down into the Atlantic Ocean. Ares would stabilize the speeder no problem, and the slick haired man would turn to you applauding and telling you all about how you should back his projects. But you wouldn't be looking at him if you were there, oh no, you'd be watching the screens, figuring out from all available data exactly where Archimedes hit the Ocean. You would have memorized the topography, it wouldn't have been that hard for you, and in a few moments of calculation, you would know everything you'd need to know, and had needed to know. You would finger your ring, the one with the sort of swirling number eight on it, and speak again.

"Well then, I think I have seen all I need to see today. Thank you." You would start towards the door, but make a sudden turn, "Oh, and I'll be needing to borrow the Ares unit, if you wouldn't mind." The slick haired man would be only too grateful, and you'd give a forced thank you.

And you would leave.

But don't worry, this won't be the last you'll see of yourself.

The Present, again

Vice handed Graelyn the tea, and she took it with a raised eyebrow at the kitten.

"So he and Ares are some crazy government program to make super soldiers, that really doesn't explain why you're here still."

"Well I didn't finish the story." She sipped the tea. "I guess the environmentalist nut-jobs were right, tea really did taste better before the ecological meltdown and the nuclear catastrophe."

"....The what?"

"Don't worry about it."

"Kind of hard to not worry about it." Graelyn gave a sort of weird plastic smile.

"You'll be dead before it happens. Oh, was that not reassuring? Darn..."

"Uh.... right, so-"

"Yes, the future."

The Future, again

Graelyn spun in her chair, letting her hair fly through the air behind her as she tried to figure out a puzzle in her head. She'd read through the library down here at project Atlantis, and with such a small staff they all had to man the sonar and scanners, which she found ludicrously dull. So dull, she didn't notice something interesting was happening at first.

"Ping," went the sonar. She spun in the chair.

"Ping," it went again. She stopped. She scooted up to the controls, and focused the various scanning systems on an object cruising down, falling more like, towards the ocean floor. She fiddled with the controls, and from Atlantis a small drone started swimming out. As the bright lights and camera of the drone focused in on the shape, she saw it was a person.

"Has to be dead." She said to no one.

"No, still alive." The drone replied back casually, "Scans show the guy is alive."

Graelyn was still a bit annoyed robots didn't talk like they did in old sci-fi movies. "How is that possible? He should be crushed by this point."

"Er, nope, looks like he's got some sort of protective suit on. Lucky, really."

"You're a robot, why were you programmed to believe in luck?"

The drone paused for a moment, "Why weren't you?" Graelyn growled.

"Don't get mad at me! Anyways, want me to bring him back in?"

Graelyn pushed her glasses firmly up the bridge of her nose towards her face.

"Affirmative."

Graelyn met the drone in the launch bay, and had it load the figure onto a gurney, which proceeded to follow Graelyn on its own power. The medical bay proved to be not particularly necessary, as scans showed the person had very little organic matter left, and the mechanical systems were already at work fixing that, but not all of those were functioning. She also learned he was biologically male (that hadn't been removed) and on a plate on the back of his head was the name "Archemedies". Graelyn grinned, and rushed him to the machine shop, where she eagerly began opening up his limbs, and fixing or replacing the broken components. When she got to his head, she unscrewed a plate to find... Computer ports. Ports into his brain. Graelyn only had a moment's hesitation of "should I?" before she began plugging cords into the man's head. It was all protected with what was the highest level security encoding, but Graelyn was eager, and she had a lot of time. She worked through the coding puzzles with glee, and began downloading the data. On her monitor were memories, repressed memories, project data.... And backed up recordings of supervised testing? She began reading, and pulling up videos. A facility full of beings like Archimedes, trained from birth to be soldiers and unaware of it... She kept going till she reached a video of a group of people watching Arch, leaping across buildings followed by a darker version of himself "Its not going as well as I thought it might." A man said.

Hours later, Archimedes woke up. He wasn't anywhere he remembered, and as he struggled to sit up, he found he couldn't.
"Shhh, its alright, just stay calm. Your name is Archimedes right?" He found he could still nod, so he did.
"You've got built in weapon systems in your limbs, and even if you didn't your arms are strong enough to literally pull me in half, so I figured it would be best to take some caution till I knew who you were."
"Who are you?" he said, his voice sounding tinny and water logged.
"Graelyn Scythes, I'm an intern here at project Atlantis."
"Never heard of it."
"I also rescued you. You had quite the fall, and you're very heavy." Archimedes had a flood of memories come back...

Ares chasing him, falling into the ocean...

"Thank you... Does anyone else know I'm here?" Graelyn shook her head.

"Most of us keep to ourselves here. We're all working on the same project, but I can't say any of us are particularly... Social. My boss wants this project done, so I'm doing it. Pays pretty well."

"Could I sit up?" Graelyn had almost forgotten.

"Oh, sure. Its not like you could get out of here alive if you tried to hurt me anyways." She wandered around his body, and made a few adjustments. "Should work now." Archimedes sat up, keenly aware that her hands had been inside his limbs. It wasn't very different than a doctor messing with your insides he supposed, but it still felt funny. He tested his fingers, and got down from the table with a "thud" that rattled the room. Graelyn took a step back.

"No need to worry, I'm not going to hurt you." She nodded, though it wasn't the most reassuring thing in the world. It was one thing to know logically someone had no reason to hurt you, and another to stand in a room next to a walking tank coated in enough airtight alloyed metal to not be crushed by the ocean, who knew you'd been messing with his servos. "Er, follow me," she said.

Graelyn lead him into a hallway filled with portraits and sculptures of various sea gods and myths. Whoever picked them out wasn't too picky, and a lot of them just had to do with water. Arch stopped to look at them.

"You alright?" He nodded, "My family raised me on Greek Mythology. They're all gone now, but I still love it myself. This one is Odysseus trying to get home, over there is

Artemis bathing and punishing the hunter who watched her, Poseidon's wrath..." He trailed off, and Graelyn wondered if patting him on the shoulder would be the appropriate response. "Never mind," he finished, "its in the past."

"I've always found the oceans fascinating, its one of the reasons I came here. Though the project itself isn't about that."

"What is it about?"

"I'll show you later for now lets just get lunch."

After lunch, Archimedes followed Graelyn through what seemed like an endless series of unmarked doors with code pads, retina readers, key card slots, DNA analysis ports, and a plethora of other security devices. For an inaccessible underwater base, the place was locked down tight.

"Is all of this really necessary?" she didn't deign that with a response, and simply stuck her arm into the slot to let the door take a blood sample. The door opened, and finally there wasn't another door. Instead there was a vast circular room, the entire wall besides the opening for the door (and another door on the room's opposite side) filled with machinery and computer mainframes. In the center of the room was what looked like a huge gyroscope that had stopped spinning in mid turn, like a photograph of a dancer in motion. Scientists were scampering around the place like ants, doing this or that job, and others were on the floor on loose blankets, taking a nap, or hastily forcing some food down. A few headed in or out of the room's other door, which was clearly the bathroom and shower. Whatever this was, it was a 24 hour operation. Near the center stood a man in an argyle sweater vest over a dress shirt, a tie loosely hanging around his neck. Despite the sign noting otherwise, he was smoking an electronic cigarette, the vapor rising up from it at regular intervals with a small blue glow.

"Who's the hunk of iron?" he asked, as though he had turned away from looking at the gyroscope.

"I think its something for a special ops project. I'm showing him around." The man nodded.

"So, what is this place?" the question caused Graelyn to grin wildly.

"This my new friend, is a portal between dimensions."

"You can make those? I thought that was something out of science fiction?" said the towering cyborg who had survived the crushing depths of the ocean.
"You can." Said the man at the center of the room.

"But really, you shouldn't." said the man who had suddenly appeared in the room along with an equally towering figure that was identical to Archimedes but black and with no coat. The man finally looked away from the gyroscope, his e-cig going limp in his lips. "How on Earth did you get in here?"
The man began looking around the room as though he was looking at a child's science fair project.

"Descent, fairly descent. You haven't stabilized the holding pattern though. Not that it matters. I'm here to shut your operation down."

Grey's boss chuckled at that, "really? On whose authority?"

"I work for a people who regulate things like this. You're about to mess with the barrier between universes, and that is something I'm afraid I simply cannot abide.

"I haven't heard of such an organization."

"A small species like yours wouldn't have."

"There's no way you can take us all down."

"Oh really? Did you forget where you are?" As if on cue, the doors began to open. All of them, all over the base. Graelyn scampered from arch to a switch board which she operated at intense speeds. Arch could hear the water coming into the base, rushing through the halls, as the gyroscope started spinning. The man who had appeared began yelling at Graelyn's boss, who yelled back, and Ares began to move towards Archimedes. Arch shifted his shoulders, and pushed out the swords loaded in his arms as Ares marched towards him, casually batting a man in a lab coat from his path as he did so. Ares' blades extended... So here it was, the final battle. He began to raise his arms in a fighting stance, and felt someone tugging on his arm. He began following the tug by rote, only to turn and see Graelyn leading him towards the spinning gyroscope which was now.... Glowing. The water surged in, smashing men and women off their feet, the yelling intensified, and Graelyn and Arch stood right in front of the spinning machine.

"Jump in it." It did not look exactly safe.

"Are you crazy?"

"We'll drown!" He felt like saying, "No, you'll drown." But then again, yes, she would drown. And whatever this was, it was dangerous. She looked at him, waiting, the water rising around her feet, Ares sloshing towards them. Arch looked at her one more time, she bit her lip, and he stepped into the spinning glow.

The Present

There comes a time in every person's life where they find themselves in their living room with a large metal cyborg and a scientist in a pencil skirt, however do to the prevalence of invisibility technologies in the future, most of us never notice these people. However, as Graelyn's story ended, the knocking on the door seemed to signal that of course, this time was drawing near for everyone involved. Graelyn was nursing her cup of tea as though it might hemorrhage if she turned away from it, and the knock on the door was loud enough Miranda was a bit worried there would be dents in the door. Vice rose up, and hesitantly turned the door knob. He supposed if it was the other cyborg trying to murder them all, it probably wouldn't be so friendly as to knock, and deluded himself with this only long enough for the lie he told himself to actually be proved completely right as Archimedes stood at the door, his shoulder dislocated and making small circular spasming motions every ten seconds or so, a crack running along his face plate and chest. He staggered in, and Vice considered trying to help him, but decided getting out of his way was the most prudent option. Arch staggered over towards where Graelyn sat, and slid down next to the couch. She took a hand away from her cup, and slid it down onto the shoulder that wasn't experiencing mechanical failure, a gesture that seemed remarkably loving despite how hard it was to remember Arch wasn't just a machine. He cursed, and pulled some cord or tube out from under the plate over his collarbone, and his right arm fell limp. There was silence.

Some moments are not filled with great dialogues, or any important information, but are all the more important because of it. There was only the four of them, who were essentially strangers, taking in the nature of their equally strange joining. Vice looked at Miranda, and for some reason they smiled, but the silence wasn't to last.
There was a knock on the door. It wasn't a normal knock, or even a shave-and-a-hair-cut knock. It was a specific four note rhythm. It repeated itself.
"Oh no..." Graelyn muttered. Her face fell.

"I'm guessing I shouldn't open the door?
Graelyn laughed. "Won't do you any good. He'll open it anyways."
The lock began to turn.
The three of them stared in silence as the lock clicked, and the door swung open, revealing Ares who was surrounded in an aura of rage as he walked in, or rather limped in, his shell coated in cracks, his left leg weighing him down like a ball and chain as there was barely any power surging through it. Then, with a small popping sound, and a whoosh, the man in the robes appeared on the loveseat,

holding what looked like a mint julep. He looked towards them with the authority the sun has to rise in the morning. "Ah, right. Universe 2345-87-Kalph. Not what I was expecting. I was really hoping you wouldn't have nachos here. But that's beside the point... You've been a very naughty girl, miss Scythes." No one squirmed. No one spoke.

"Its been a long time since I was in a parallel universe," he continued as though he was at a pleasant garden party, and sipped his drink, "you know, most of them aren't very different. I once had to chronicle ten million universes that were all a variation on how one dog sneezed at one point in history. Almost nothing was ever different, least important sneeze in history as it turns out. This one at least has the Kentucky Derby on Earth, would you believe they hold it in Dallas on some worlds?"

There surely was a correct response to what had just been said, and someone somewhere knew what it was, but that person was certainly not in the room with Vice, Miranda, Arch, and Graelyn. They all just took their chance to stare.

"Well, talkative bunch. I'm afraid though this is the end of the line for all of you. You've broken the laws of time, space, and some other things to. It's all quite terrible. Luckily for me, the two of you," he gestured towards the couch with his cup, sloshing it a bit, "won't even need to go through judicial proceedings. All I have to do is restore you to your regular universe where you left off, and your lack of gills will take care of the rest."

"I just worked there, you tried to kill us all. I just wanted to learn."

"Well, you're not ready to learn that."

"Who says?"

"Me." The finality of declaring oneself arbiter and executioner is an empowering one, but also a highly limiting one. After all, if one is not on good terms with one's arbiter, one is not particularly keen to follow their lead, and if one has just made tea for guests, even giving out the kitty cup, watching someone say they will drown your guests is unpleasant. Vice quickly made an inspection of the situation.

He had guests from another universe, and some sort of inter-dimensional sheriff.

"But how did he get here?" He thought to himself. He looked the man over: he was middle aged, but his eyes looked much older. He was wearing robes with designs he didn't recognize, a sort of skull cap, and an armband. Vice decided that anyone with the power to hop into his living room from nowhere with a mint julep probably wouldn't like witnesses around, and so there wasn't much to lose in doing something very stupid, so naturally Vice did something really dumb. Two things, actually.

First, he grabbed the pink mug with the kitties out of Graelyn's grip, and threw the still hot tea at the man in the skullcap. The man was so shocked he barely noticed as Vice rushed forward and grabbed at the man's armband. He gave a little yelp, and then neither of them were in the room at all.

France, 1832
Jean looked over at Marcel, "Its no good, the national guard will be upon us by morning." Marcel nodded sadly, "I'd hoped the revolution would spread like wildfire, but I see we were just a candl-" it was just then that two men rolled out of thin air with a pop and a whoosh and fell next to them on top of the barricade. They were dressed…. Very oddly, though one might have been a clergy man, abeit not a Catholic one certainly. "Let go, you don't know what you're playing with!" the protestant yelled. "graaahhhhG!" yelled the other man, as he pulled an armband off of the man with such force he fell down the barricade, bruising himself on a few chairs.

"Monsieur, are you alright?" Jean yelled down. The priest was already charging down the barricade, and the other man dizzily looked up at Jean, "You might want to leave, 1848 will go a lot better!" and then the priest grabbed the armband, and pop! They were gone. The two comrades looked at each other, and quietly decided to go home and get some wine.

Cardiff, Wales 1972
A dog sneezed. Two men rolled through the grass next to it, and then disappeared. The dog looked for something to eat.

Articulanthererium, 4578
Ellen 14 was having trouble today, the other clones just were not listening and they were never going to get the harvest in, she sighed, and then two men fell in front of her yelling, and promptly disappeared, then reappeared. One

kicked the other, and stumbled away cursing holding a small hollow ring. The other stumbled up and hit some buttons on the giant harvester no one knew how to work-- it roared to life, and began rushing towards the man with the ring, who dodged out of the way, letting the first man tackle him, and they disappeared again. The machine began harvesting the fields. She leaned back in her chair, okay day after all.

The future, New Moscow
Graelyn ran across the field as the great rolling disks that transported the Hererium tumbled through the deep trenches to her right. She liked to race the disks, study them, but today was different; there was a pair of men in her path fighting over a fancy looking bracelet. Her parents had always told her not to share. She tried to figure out how to explain to the two men that they should resolve their want of the bracelet in a different way-- but then one looked at her and said, "Greyl-" and they both vanished. Another disk rolled by.

Somewhere else, Some when else
They rolled away from each other, tumbling off of the dais they had landed on. Vice scampered up, and ran towards the bracelet, but found he was running in place... and so was the man.
"STOP."
Okay, stop. Vice could do that. Stopping. He was all about stopping. He'd started all of this by going for a walk, stopping was probably a pretty great idea.
"Neither of you you should be here." The voice repeated,

not quite so loud or booming. Vice got himself oriented: he was in a room on a dais that was surrounded by a pit, and the pit surrounded by a high wall atop which there were many thrones, in which he could tell there were beings seated in... But between the darkness around them and pinpoint blinding light directed at him, he couldn't quite make out their features. There were strange smells, and ambient noises... Vice got the distinct impression that these were to disorient him as well, to prevent him from seeing the beings sitting above him. Which was a bit rude of hosts, really. He was contained in some sort of invisible bubble, and floating in the air. This was extremely abnormal, and after everything else today, Vice was getting a bit tired of running into strange and unusual things he didn't understand.

"This is... This is the council. Let me out, I'm simply doing my job, for you!"

"Am I?" replied the same voice, only it didn't come from the man in the robes. A figure leaned in, pushing his face into view of the light-- it was the same man, or so it looked like.

"Actually, it looks like you, or I, my apologies, are interfering in the policies of another universe. Frankly, I'm embarrassed for myself."

Vice looked between them, "So, you're like... The time cops?"

"Nothing so banal or crass as that. Our right is genetic, hereditary."

Vice nodded, "right, great. But you're all about law and order right? No funny business."

"Humor is a misdemeanor."

"Great! So clearly he is in the wrong, has taken me away from my native home and time, and I need to be put back there, and Archimedes and Graelyn should be taken back home." The shadowy figures grumbled.

"I'm afraid not, they are criminals, messing with time and space is an offense." Vice looked around the ornate room trying to think of something. Everything was ordered. Everything was in its place.

"But you have to respect the sovereign rules of different worlds right?"

"...Go on."

"Well, I grant Archimedes and Graelyn asylum on Earth." The man in the robes, who was now staring at Vice open mouthed, let out a fit of anger, flailing his limbs in the air.

"No! He can't do that! You won't let him do that, will I?"

"This human has the right to take in asylum seekers."

"Great. Now I formally request assistance getting them home."

The room let out a long sigh.

"Fine. We'll have Lady Aesculapius take them there. She's always into that kind of thing. You're dismissed."

The man let out an angry diatribe, but the other of him silenced himself.

"And I hereby condemn myself to subspace prison until I think I have learned my lesson."

"Oh come on, I wouldn't do that to myself!"

"I just did."

Vice sighed as he was teleported out, alternate realities were sure a bother.

Earth, the Present

Vice fell back onto the floor of the living room, everyone in exactly the places they had been when he left. Ares stopped his slow trudge.

"Vice...?" Miranda piqued up.

Vice gave a tired thumbs up.

"Good news everyone, you're all going home, and that guy is in jail."

There was a storm of questions, and Vice waved it off, "I'll explain later...." he muttered. He got up off the floor. Ares was staring at him, "and what of me?"

"You can go home to. Just don't bother us again. Ever." Ares gave a slow nod.

As soon as he said that, there was a noise, like the whoosh the armband made, only longer and deeper, and a grand piano appeared in the room. The lid popped open, and a woman in a bow-tie, frock coat, blouse, long skirt, and a flat top cap crawled out of it.

"Hello, I'm lady Aesculapius, I hear you need a lift?"

"Did you just fly that piano in here?" She looked down at her piano, and laughed.

"Well I can't easily fit inside a flute, can I? Let alone take on passengers. So what, just next universe over?"

"I suppose so," Graelyn answered, if that one is home." She just shrugged in response, "I'll get you there eventually. Might be the fourth try."

Graelyn helped Arch up, and the two made their way into the Piano, followed slowly by Ares.

"Thank you so much, both of you," Archimedes said as he walked past vice and Miranda, and Graelyn gave a short smile and wave. Ares didn't say anything. The piano disappeared as quickly as it had come. Miranda and Vice looked around their living room, which was suddenly far too normal and far too empty.

"Wait a second," Vice realized, "she stole the kitty cup."

Six months later.

Vice and Miranda sat at the coffee shop, thumbing through a single newspaper between the two of them. Vice looked out the window, and a man walked by with a dog. The dog sneezed.

"Mind if I join you?" both looked up. Both saw Graelyn Scythes, only dressed quite a bit fancier. Both stood up.

"Oh don't get worried, for me this is only a week after I saw you last. Unfortunately we've been having an awkward trip getting home. But we ended up here, so I thought I'd say goodbye properly from the future."

"I wan-"

"You're not getting the mug back."

"Then why are you here?" Miranda asked.

"To tell you that this place you live in matters. You've both seen quite a lot of things, metal men falling out of holes in the sky... Vice you saw other worlds and times, and you might think this world you live in is drab now, you might even think it doesn't matter since its just one of many worlds people live in... But you live here, and that matters."

"We're not particularly special you know."

Graelyn just laughed, "Special enough you know not only about the universe around you, but that a mug with kitties on it is better than one without them."

Miranda shook her head, "That just means we have bad taste."

"No, it means you do what you like, you enjoy your life, and aren't afraid to help others when the need for it comes. You aren't afraid to just... Be who you are, enjoy what you like whether its popular or cool or legitimized by some council. You are yourselves, and you shouldn't change that. Enjoy the mugs with kitties on them, that's the best advice I can give you."

"That's the worst advice I ever heard." Miranda said.

Graelyn just shrugged, and walked out the door.

"Think she had a point?" Vice shrugged.

"I think if you think it does, it does." Miranda mulled that over.

"Then I changed my mind. Lets go for a walk."

"Don't you know walks are dangerous?"

"Then lets live dangerously."

They stepped out into the cool morning air, and found that they were going on exactly the kind of walk one does when someone is about to do something amazing.

9 AFTERWORD

50 years ago, a crazy Sci-Fi show about an old man and his granddaughter who were on the run from their own time and accidentally kidnapped her school teachers went on the air, and somehow ended up going straight into our hearts.

Because it was wonderful, inspiring, and absolutely insane.

So thank you for joining me on this journey of Eloquence through Time and Space, its been a pleasure.

As a final treat, after writing hundreds of pages of poetry I wrote a parody of my own writing, and after reading this book I thought you might get a smirk out of it yourself:

A Summation of This Book
Cold opening
Trojan War Imagery
simile or metaphor
intentional mysssphelling
rhetorical question?
Play on words from TV

Space to create dramatic tension

a final line that is pseudo-meaningful

For the convenience of those Kickstarter Backers who commissioned a poem from me, here is a handy index for where they can be located in the book:

Happy 50th Anniversary to all Doctor Who fans everywhere!
-Jim Wylder

ABOUT THE AUTHOR

James Wylder has been writing since he was a child, and has had the crazy luck to have a few plays produced, some poetry published, and basically have his dreams come true.

His first memory of Doctor Who is the 2nd Doctor Serial "The Seeds of Death" which he re-enacted with Legos and shaving cream, much to his parents chagrin as they had to clean it up.

James lives in Elkhart Indiana where he works as a substitute teacher, and enjoys writing, running, reading, and roleplaying games.

He also has a really awesome girlfriend he deeply loves, and is not sucking up to her at all with with this sentence.

32959193R00287

Made in the USA
Charleston, SC
29 August 2014